My Story with Science and Technology Backyards in China

Some Experience from Sino-Africa STB Project

我和科技小院的故事

非洲版

郭宇 姜姗 编

化学工业出版社

·北京·

内 容 简 介

科技小院是建立在农村生产一线，集科技创新、人才培养和示范推广于一体的基层科技服务平台，由研究生和教授常年紧密联系农业生产一线，解决农业研究与生产应用脱节、农业人才培养与农业生产结合不紧密、农业技术转化效果差的问题，并在生产一线开展实用技术创新。

将科技小院培养模式应用到非洲高校人才培养体系中，了解非洲农业生产需求，适应非洲农业生产一线的工作，将中国先进农业技术应用于非洲并进行创新，培养知华、友华、爱华、亲华的高素质人才，大范围地服务非洲地区农业、农村和农民，改善民生条件和水平，推动非洲地方经济发展。

本书描述了非洲留学生在科技小院的成长历程与故事，记录了他们扎根农业生产一线过程中的所见、所闻、所思，通过以科技小院模式培养非洲研究生的新做法，探索了服务非洲农业绿色发展的机制。

图书在版编目（CIP）数据

我和科技小院的故事：非洲版=My Story with Science and Technology Backyards in China——Some Experience from Sino-Africa STB Project：英文/郭宇，姜姗编. —北京：化学工业出版社，2022.9

ISBN 978-7-122-41612-4

Ⅰ.①我… Ⅱ.①郭…②姜… Ⅲ.①中国农业大学-研究生-社会实践-非洲-英文 Ⅳ.①G643

中国版本图书馆CIP数据核字（2022）第107611号

责任编辑：李建丽
责任校对：杜杏然
装帧设计：李子姮

出版发行：化学工业出版社
　　　　　（北京市东城区青年湖南街13号　邮政编码100011）
印　　装：中煤（北京）印务有限公司
710mm×1000mm　1/16　印张13¼　彩插7　字数256千字
2024年4月北京第1版第1次印刷

购书咨询：010-64518888
售后服务：010-64518899
网　　址：http://www.cip.com.cn
凡购买本书，如有缺损质量问题，本社销售中心负责调换。

定　　价：69.00元

前　言

　　让研究生驻扎在生产一线，与村民同住在村中的小院里，这可不是简单短暂的体验生活，他们三年研究生中大半时间是在这里学习、锻炼、成长。在为当地农民办讲座、解决生产问题、做服务的同时，也完成了自己的研究任务和学位论文，培养了自身吃苦耐劳的精神，以及发现实际问题、分析问题、解决问题的能力。这就是由中国农业大学资源与环境学院张福锁院士团队2009年在全国首创的科技小院工作模式。科技小院是建立在农村生产一线，集科技创新、人才培养和示范推广于一体的基层科技服务平台，由研究生和教授常年紧密联系农业生产一线，解决农业研究与生产应用脱节、农业人才培养与农业生产结合不紧密、农业技术转化效果差的问题，并在生产一线开展实用技术创新。

　　如今我们将进一步丰富科技小院培养模式，将集农业科技创新、社会服务和人才培养于一体的人才培养模式推广到国际化、创新型留学人才的培养中。以多学科教学、科研平台来推动非洲国家农业人才培养－技术示范－产品生产和推广机制建设。通过将科技小院培养模式移植到非洲高校人才培养体系中，了解非洲农业生产需求，适应非洲农业生产一线的工作，将中国先进农业技术应用于非洲并进行创新，培养知华、友华、爱华、亲华的高素质人才，大范围服务非洲地区农业、农村和农民，改善民生条件和水平，推动非洲地方经济发展。

　　本书以留学生作为讲述者，他们用最真实的文字，向身边乃至世界范围内对"中非科技小院"感兴趣的人们，诉说他们在中国的故事，展现最真实的样貌和他们最真切的感触。同时本书也是让更多的人认识科技小院模式，了解"中非科技小院"的媒介。

　　本书由来自非洲八个国家（埃塞俄比亚、尼日利亚、赞比亚、津巴布韦、莫桑比克、坦桑尼亚、塞内加尔、布基纳法索）的22名中非科技小院项目（Sino-Africa STB Project）研究生撰写，另外由中非科技小院项目学生助管郭宇、姜姗担任编者，留学生们以本书为窗口分享他们在中国学习的经历与见闻。同时本书也是根据中非科技小院项目的留学生在中国实践案例报告编写的，旨在为大家留下一份难忘的回忆。

本书从征稿到整理出版历时较长时间，中间经过多次修改与完善。也得到了许多老师们宝贵的建议。

因此，在这里特别感谢张福锁院士、江荣风教授、焦小强副教授以及中国农业大学资源与环境学院植物营养系各位老师的悉心指导。他们在很多方面给予了宝贵的建议，为了保证本书顺利、高质量的完成出版，花费了大量的工作和业余时间，再次表达衷心的感谢和敬意。

由于编者水平有限，书中难免存在不足之处，敬请读者批评指正。

编 者

Preface

Having postgraduate students live at the front line of production and living with villagers in a small courtyard in the village is not simply a short experience of life—they spend most of their three years as postgraduate students here to learn, exercise and grow. While giving lectures, solving production problems and providing services to local farmers, they also completed their research tasks and graduation thesis, and cultivated their spirit of hardship and hard work, as well as their ability to find practical problems, analyze them and solve them. This is the work model of STB pioneered by the team of academician Zhang Fusuo from the College of Resources and Environment of China Agricultural University in 2009 in China. It is a grass roots science and technology service platform established at the front line of rural production, integrating science and technology innovation, talent cultivation and demonstration and promotion, with postgraduates and professors in close contact with the front line of agricultural products all year round, solving the problems of disconnection between agricultural research and production application, poor integration between agricultural talent cultivation and agricultural production, and poor transformation of agricultural technology, and carrying out practical technological innovation at the front line of production.

Now we will further enrich the cultivation model

of the STB and extend the talent cultivation model integrating agricultural science and technology innovation, social service and talent cultivation to the cultivation of international and innovative overseas talents. We will use the multidisciplinary teaching and research platform to promote the construction of the mechanism of agricultural talent cultivation, technology demonstration, product production and promotion in African countries. By transplanting the training model of STB into the talent training system of African universities, the students will understand the needs of agricultural production in Africa, adapt to the front-line work of agricultural production in Africa, apply Chinese advanced agricultural technology in Africa and make innovations cultivate high-quality talents who know China, befriend China, love China and are pro-China, serve the agriculture, rural areas and farmers in Africa on a large scale, improve the conditions and level of people's livelihood, and promote local economic development in Africa.

The book uses international students as narrators to tell their stories in China to people around them and the world who are interested in the "Sino-Africa Science and Technology Backyard", showing the most realistic pictures and their most sincere feelings. The book also serves as a medium for more people to get to know the model and the "Sino-Africa Science and Technology Backyard".

This book is written by 22 graduate students from

eight African countries (Ethiopia, Nigeria, Zambia, Zimbabwe, Mozambique, Tanzania, Senegal, and Burkina Faso) in the Sino-Africa STB Project, and edited by Guo Yu and Jiang Shan, student assistants of the Sino-Africa STB Project. This is a book about the experiences and insights of the international students studying in China. It is also written as a case report of international students' practice in China for Sino-Africa STB Project, which can leave a precious memory for everyone.

This book took a long time from the call for papers to the publication, and was revised and improved many times. It has also received many valuable suggestions from teachers.

Therefore, we would like to express our special thanks to academician Zhang Fusuo, Professor Jiang Rongfeng, Associate Professor Jiao Xiaoqiang, and teachers of the Department of Plant Nutrition. They have given valuable advice in many aspects and spent a lot of their time, both during work and in their spare time, to ensure the smooth and high-quality completion of this book for publication.

Editors

Contents

Mudare Shingirai

"Above all, I will never forget that they treated us with a lot of respect and they are also willing to learn from us. We exchanged a lot of things, such as stories to moments, and I learned a lot about cultural differences. In every experience I got from the county I would also want to acknowledge the student-teacher relationship of mine that improved as I stayed at Quzhou Experimental Station. We had experts like Professor Rongfeng, Professor Hongyan, and Professor Xiaoqiang. Several other professors would occasionally come to the station and share their expertise with us and return to Beijing. Quzhou will always be at my heart because it was the first place for me to do an online presentation and hold classes online. I will never forget this great experience in my lifetime."

Mudare Shingirai is a young man aged 29 from Zimbabwe. He is currently studying for a Master of Science degree in Resource Utilization, Environmental Science, and Plant Protection at China Agricultural University with the College of Resources and Environmental Sciences. His major experiences include farm and agribusiness management, particularly preparing farm budgets. He is a crop scientist who has experience in growing maize, tobacco, potatoes, and several vegetables. In animal husbandry, he has worked with Red Dane farm, one of the biggest dairy farms in Zimbabwe where he raised calves, took care of heifers and steers, managed artificial insemination, animal feeding, and the milking parlor. He also has practical experience in farm machinery and workshop management. Previously he worked for the Ministry of Primary and Secondary Education as a teacher in agriculture at all levels.

His motto: No greatness without hard work.

Amani Stephen Milinga

"I came to realize that China has invested hugely in agricultural research so as to come up with solutions for the real challenges facing smallholders and agriculture as a sector. I have also learned that, if the younger generation like us are exposed to the high-level agricultural training like this one, it will attract and motivate more and more young people to participate in agricultural research or work in the area of agricultural expertise and the agricultural production chain."

Amani Stephen Milinga joined China Agricultural University as a professional graduate student in the College of Resources and Environmental Sciences in 2019. Prior to coming to China, he served as Agriculture Officer at the Department of Agriculture and Extension Services of the Tanzania Smallholders Tea Development Agency (TSHTDA) in Tanzania. Amani received his Bachelor of Science in Agriculture General from the Sokoine University of Agriculture, Morogoro, Tanzania, in 2013 and is currently pursuing Master of Science in Resources & Environmental Sciences and Plant Protection at China Agricultural University as a member of Science and Technology Backyard (STB) programme.

Amani's agricultural interests include training tea smallholders in good agricultural practices, sustainable agriculture and environmental protection. He worked with tea farmers in Tanzania for five years and in 2017 he was certified as Tea Master level five (5) by the Ministry of Human Resources and Social Security of the People's Republic of China. His primary research interests lie in the field of sustainable agriculture and crop productivity.

Bilisuma Kabeto Wako

"There were eight courses in the first semester: elementary Chinese, organic farming, efficient utilization of agri-produce, nonpoint source pollution of agriculture, thesis writing, biometrics and experimental design, rural revitalization and innovation and research integrity and academic norms. These courses were managed by one professor, but taught by different professors from the same university and different companies. The course was also supported by excursion which made our learning process more fruitful. It was a very interesting and joyful time for studying.**"**

Bilisuma Kabeto Wako comes from Oromia region, Ethiopia. He graduated from Haramaya University in 2014 majored in rural development and agricultural extension. He worked as junior and assistant researcher of agricultural extension research in Oromia Agricultural Research Institute for more than three and a half years. During his stay in Oromia Agricultural Research Institute, he had worked as the team leader of agricultural extension and coordinator of socio-economics and agricultural extension research process. He also worked as the focal person of HIV and gender, coordinating and giving training on crosscutting issues. Now, Bilisuma is pursuing his post graduate study at China Agricultural University in the major of resource utilization and plant protection. After graduation, Bilisuma plans to serve the farmers in his country Ethiopia with the knowledge and skills he gained at China Agricultural University.

Buana Suefo

" Every student has their own unique story, and each story consists of many sometimes small, sometimes great, but all different and interesting experiences. We enjoy learning experiences from other people, here is my story, I hope you'll enjoy it too. "

His name is Buana Suefo. He is a Sino-Africa STB master student from the College of Environmental Science, majoring in resource utilization and plant protection in China Agricultural University (CAU). from 2011 to 2019 he was a formatter at the Institute Polytechnic of Nacuxa, supported by Ministry of Science and Technology in Mozambique.

Working Experience in China

P31-P38

Erick Emmanuel Kumari

"The campus life in Chinese universities is rich, colorful, and fulfilling. You will find campus life in China vibrant and welcoming with many opportunities to get involved in events and activities that might attract and interest you. Nearly all the universities have offered various fully equipped facilities for the convenience of students for spare time sports activities. When international students decide to study in China, they are embarking on a new journey of study life and steping out from their comfort zone. They will be trained to be more independent, flexible, enjoy the unexpected and meet new people and cultures from many countries around them."

Erick Emmanuel Kumari is an agripreneur and currently a graduate student at China Agricultural University, Beijing, China. Holding a bachelor's degree in horticulture from Sokoine University of Agriculture, Morogoro, Tanzania, Erick excels in developing a comprehensive digital strategy to communicate and do business with agripreneurs in Tanzania. Strong organization skills, active listening skills, energetic work attitude is a sharp problem solver, adaptive and high performing team spirit, with extensive experience from Tanzania, Israel, United States of America and China.

Christina Lemson Hambo

"Staying in China and pursuing my studies at such a university was the best option and most wonderful experience in my life. The relationship between teachers and students is wonderful and well organized. All the teachers and professors are so cooperative and helpful to students. All students are encouraged to learn and participate in different university activities like cultural and academic exchange, workshops and different international conferences for their career development."

Christina Lemson Hambo, 26 years old, born in Mbeya, Tanzania, holds a BSc. Agriculture General from Sokoine University of Agriculture. She is currently a Master student at China Agricultural University pursuing MSc. Resources, Environmental Science and Plant Protection.

Her motto: Integrity and working smart for high quality output.

Experience: She is equipped with enough knowledge and skills on agriculture sector and other related fields which come from lectures, practical sessions, excursions and different international workshops. Additionally, she has worked as sales manager at Meru Agro Tours and Consultant Company Ltd. and as Program Officer at Frolesta, a non-government organization under Environmental Restoration Department.

Her smart working, integrity and self-discipline has enabled her to participate in different international workshops in China, to mention just a few: as the guest speaker at The Road and Cooperation of Science and Technology Organization Conference with the topic "Ecological Restoration in Africa", Youth Leadership Dialogue: China – Africa Agricultural Cooperation Conference, International Webinar-Earth Day: "The way forward to Climate and Health (COVID 19) and then, The 6th Global Youth Leadership Program 2020; Nurturing Leaders, Transforming Lives.

Ngula David Muttendango

"As we reached and interacted with the farmers, I couldn't get a single word. I thought I could understand mandarin as I had taken a course in my previous semester. However, the farmer's mandarin was so strange that I could barely understand. We went into the meeting place; I could remember vividly what I had read in articles and what I was seeing. The farmer field school comprised of 25-30 farmers mixed young and old, male and female. As the proceedings went on, farmers showed close attention to the presentation of the beautiful MSc student."

Ngula David Muttendango was born in Livingstone, Zambia. He got his bachelor's degree at the University of Zambia, and majored in crop science. He also participated in the one-year Agrostudies rigorous agricultural internship in Israel where he was exposed to hands-on farm management training. He is currently pursuing his master's degree at China Agricultural University, majoring in resource utilization and plant protection. His dream is to create a vertically integrated business model that will involve goat farming at the heart of the company business.

My experience in Quzhou County at Quzhou Experimental Station

Jasper Kanomanyanga

"The classes were interactive as every students had to participate in practicing to speak Chinese in front of the class. Pinyin and characters were taught during the whole semester and I managed to grasp a lot which helped me to easily adapt to the Chinese people. After about three months of learning Chinese, I could now speak with the Chinese people on different occasions like the restaurant and market although with some difficulties, and this allowed me to practice it further as I believe that practice makes perfect. **"**

Born and raised in the streets of Harare, Zimbabwe, Jasper Kanomanyanga is 28 years of old. He pursued his first degree in Agricultural Crop Science at the University of Zimbabwe and completed it in 2016. Soon after his graduation, Jasper worked for the Cotton Company of Zimbabwe (COTTCO Pvt, Ltd) from 2016 to 2019 as an extension agent and later as an area manager. It has been his core dream to attain a foreign degree from a world-renowned university and this encouraged him to start applying for international scholarships until he was accepted by the China Agricultural University (CAU) under the Chinese Council Scholarship. Currently, he is studying for Master in Science degree in Resource Utilization, Environmental Science and Plant Protection in the College of Resources and Environmental Sciences at CAU, Beijing, China (2019—2022).

The first appearance on Chinese soil—a dream turned into reality

P66-P80

Derara Sori Feyisa

"Fortunately my supervisor was living with us in the station since he is the coordinator of the program. Really I would like to appreciate his motivation in helping the students. He is energetic and dynamic person very much interested in creating good citizen. To be honest he inspired me to do many thing with great motivation. He wants all students to study hard, work hard which is very ecouragable. As general life in Quzhou Experimental station was very interesting and a place I learned a lot. Finally I would like to thank Quzhou Experimental Station's staff for their kind support in particular and China government for the opportunity we are given in general. I hope the experience that we have been sharing will bring positive change on enhancing the income of subsistent African farmers and the issue of food insecurity challenging African continent."

He is Derara Sori Feyisa from Ethiopia. He is a university graduate in rural development and agricultural extension from Haramaya University. He worked as assistant researcher in Ethiopian Institute of Agricultural Research before coming to China. Four years later, he got the opportunity to pursue master's degree in resource utilization and plant protection for three years in China Agricultural University, Beijing, China.

Priscilla Tijesuni Adisa

"I enjoyed every bit of the Chinese from the written aspect to the oral aspect. I was able to acquire knowledge of basic vocabulary needed for day-to-day activities. The first word I learnt was 'Hello – Ni Hao'. Through the course I was able to learn several conversations needed when I visit supermarkets, restaurants and banks. It was an exciting experience for me. In addition to this, Research Integrity and Academic Norms provided me with highly expository knowledge norms and misconducts in academic research which has been of great use to me in my current research."

Priscilla Tijesuni Adisa, a graduate student of College of Resource and Environmental Science, China Agricultural University. She is from Nigeria.

Motto: Rome was not built in a day, but it was laying bricks every hour.

Odigie Eromosele

" After much discussion with my supervisor, he had some concerns with my proposed experimental work, so he suggested runing a trial experiment, which I did. The pre-experiment was carried out in the greenhouse in Quzhou Experimental Station, 5 treatments with 4 replications, the treatments were 0, 30, 60, 90, 120. Every step of the experiment was studied properly and discussed with my supervisor to ensure a good result. "

Odigie Eromosele is from Nigeria, and he graduated from Federal University of Technology Minna, with a bachelor's degree in Agric and Bio-Resources Engineering. He worked at the Federal Capital Development Authority (FCDA) as a project staff (temporary staff). He plays basketball and coaches kids as a trainer at the Titans Basketball Academy in Abuja Nigeria. He is a bodybuilder, a photographer and occasionally motivator. He loves to explore new things and visit new places. He also loves to travel and take amazing photos of his exploration.

Tefera Merga

"I learn many things from my practical education and acquired knowledge like how to measure plant growth indicators and critical period to take indicator samples for different crops and hard working to achieve my goal. I get hardworking habit from Chinese farmers. They are punctual with their work and also they respect foreigners."

Tefera Merga was from Ethiopia. He was born and raised in a small rural community in Southwest-central Ethiopia. He was 29 years old and he completed his early education in his native country including a BSc in Plant Science from Mizan Tepi University in 2012. He worked for five years as an instructor at Holeta Polytechnic College. He came to China on September 14, 2019 to continue his education in master of resource utilization and plant protection. He conducted research on the effect of liquid cattle manure on yield of maize (*Zea mays*, L.) to solve the effects of chemical fertilizer and to use animal manure as a fertilizer to reduce environmental pollution.

Solomon Yokamo

"It is supposed that Chinese agricultural technology best fits for modernize African subsistence agriculture. Science and Technology Backyard is the model that links the farming and science community and other stakeholders together for mutual benefit in technology generation and dissemination. After I came to Quzhou, I have visited many STBs and crops and learned about very astonishing technologies in different agricultural production systems."

Solomon Yokamo was born in Ethiopia in one of the rural areas in Sidama region, Shebedino Woreda on 11th Sept 1993. He joined Wolaita Sodo University (WSU) in Ethiopia from 2012 to 2014 under the school of Agriculture at the Department of Rural Development & Agricultural Extension (RDAE). After graduation, he worked in Shebedino Woreda urban development and housing sector as an urban agriculture officer for one and a half years. Then after, he worked in the South Agricultural Research Institute (SARI) under Arbaminch Agricultural Research Centre (AMARC) as an agricultural technology transfer researcher from May 2016. His major role in the research centre was providing training to the farmers & development personnel and conducting demonstration plots on farmers field and FTCs to enhance technology adoption and recording & share the results with science community. He got the CSC scholarship opportunity and came to China on 8th Sept 2019 and became the student of CAU under the College of Resources and Environmental Science.

Lawal Olusola Lawal

"It is interesting for me to note my meeting with the head of Wangzhuang village during one of my visits to the village for farmer's survey. He's a complete gentleman who is full of energy and very sweet personality. He also happens to be a farmer himself and after answering my questionnaire, he also helped me in encouraging some of his friends that are farmers to do same."

Lawal Olusola Lawal comes from Nigeria. He gets the bachelor's degree of Agriculture.

In line with the plan and objectives of the Sino-Africa STB program which is to develop technology innovation and knowledge transfer in rural area with the STB model and empower smallholder farmers in Africa, he is meant to stay in Quzhou Experimental Station in order to acquire some practical skills and experience in sustainable agriculture, learn more about the STB model and carry out experiments, researches and farmers' survey.

During his stay here, he was able to carry out a farmer's survey for his research titled "Assessment of challenges limiting the use of manure among smallholder farmers in Quzhou county of China". A structured questionnaire which has been carefully translated into Chinese language was used to collect primary data from 120 participants (farmers) who were randomly selected from two different STB villages (Wangzhuang and Fuzhuang) in the study area. The farmer's survey (data collection) was done with the support of Chinese partners attached to him by his supervisor, Professor Cui Zhenling.

The most precious moment during his six months stay in rural China was that he was able to interact and carry out a successful farmer's survey among local Chinese farmers despite cultural and language barriers that exist. This is a very precious experience for him because it has provided him with a very rare opportunity as an agricultural extension agent from Africa (Nigeria) to have first-hand experience of what it looks and takes for a non-Chinese speaker to carry out a farmer's survey study in China.

Philippe Yameogo

"My days at Quzhou Experimental Station were noted by self-study session and the participation of seminars. The comfortableness of the study room offers me a favourable condition to concentrate on my literature research and my daily writing (Photo 11). This situation of self-study has increasingly improved my capacity of reading, analysing and summarizing of scientific papers."

Philippe Yameogo is from Burkina Faso, a country which means "land of honest men". He is 33 years old. With a basic training in earth science, he joined the Ministry of Agriculture with a degree in agricultural engineering. With his profile of agriculture engineer, he worked as an extension agent at the Regional Extension Service of Plateau Centre where he held many functions. From the responsibility of the compiling, monitoring/evaluating and managing of the department activities, he became the central agent of the National Program of Vulgarization and Advice Support Agricultural with the mission of coordinating and planning of the activities of popularization and agricultural advice support.

His experience in China is reflected in his familiarization with Chinese practices and millet production technics. The discovery of new technologies used on the production of the wheat, apple and grape through the visit and training in the villages of Science and Technology Backyard gave him a new vision of agriculture.

Motto: Self-confidence is the best companion.

Teodósio Titos Leonardo Macuácua

"On the other hand, for the success of Sino-AFRICA STB in my country, as it would do so to connect the scientific community to the agricultural community to facilitate the exchange of information and innovations. Science-based management technologies are brought in by the STB team and discussed with leading farmers, the latter providing feedback that is then addressed, resulting in recommendations applicable to the holding."

Teodósio Titos Leonardo Macuácua, 27 years old of Mozambican nationality, is a high school teacher in Agriculture. He holds a Bachelor's Degree in Agricultural Production from the Eduardo Mondlane University (UEM) of Mozambique, and a formation in Agricultural Sciences and Agrarian Mechanization from the IF-Federal Institute of Brazil.

He has four years of work experience as a trainer in the areas of agricultural mechanization, planning, and analysis of small agricultural projects, agricultural machinery maintenance, communication, and rural extension. He is a developer of agricultural projects, planning, and analysis at Três Rios Agricultura LDA company.

He is currently at the College of Resources and Environmental Sciences of China Agricultural University (CAU). He is one of the students of the first promotion of the Sino-Africa Science and Technology Backyard (STB) Project for a Master in Resources Utilization and Plant Protection. For this Training, he dedicated himself to Soil Management and Environmental Protection. His search topic is "Effects of synthetic nitrogen fertilizer and composted chicken manure on ammonia (NH_3) volatilization in winter wheat-summer maize rotation system.

Igbinedion Rosemary Izehiuwa

"My stay at Quzhou has been of great benefit and impact. I have learned some improved agronomic practices and ways in which smallholder farmers can improve their yield. I researched literature relating to my thesis during my leisure period when I'm not on the field or having lectures. My most memorable day in Quzhou was when I finally harvested my maize field."

Igbinedion Rosemary Izehiuwa, from Nigeria, 32 years old, is currently a master's student of China Agricultural University, College of Resources and Environmental Sciences. She majors in Resources Utilization, Environmental Science and Plant Protection.

Her motto: Life is tough but so are you, make your life a master piece; imagine no limitations on what you can be, have or do.

Theobard Stephano
Chagga

"It is my hope that, as days go by, we will fulfill our goal of learning the best ways to cooperate with smallholder farmers in order to find solutions to various challenges in the process of crop production, which will ultimately impact agriculture in Africa as we will take this new knowledge and experience back home and use it to benefit our societies. Lastly, I would like to appreciate the warm welcome, assistance and cooperation from STB administrators."

Prior to joining China Agricultural University (CAU), he was working with a private entrepreneurial organization that was specialized in the transfer of agricultural knowledge to various groups of people in society including women, agricultural graduates, and anyone from any sector and background interested in modern and sustainable farming. He got his Bachelor degree in horticulture from Sokoine University of Agriculture in Tanzania in 2016. After graduation, he had participated in various training and internship programs to further improve his knowledge in agriculture particularly practical skills. He participated in agriculture internship in Israel from October 2016 to October 2017. Also, he went on to pursue another agriculture internship in the United States for six months from April to October 2018. After that he joined a private enterprise associated in dissemination of farming knowledge to different groups as he mentioned earlier until the opportunity to study in China came about.

Wakjira Gurmesa Djano

> "In Quzhou Experimental Station I have got a lot of experience. That season was the winter season and the North China Plain is known for producing winter wheat. There were a different activity on the field, especially how they used different fertilizers such as phosphorous, Nitrogen, and mixed ones."

Wakjira Gurmesa Djano was born in 1988 in West Wollega, Oromia region, Ethiopia. In 2009 he joined Arba Minch University and graduated with BSc in animal science in 2011. After graduation, he was employed as a Holeta Poly Technic College Instructor at the Department of Animal Science in 2015. His main duties were giving training for students, preparing learning and teaching materials, and giving different local community services according to Ethiopian Techincal and Vocational Institute policy. Later on, after six-year services for his local communities, he got another opportunity that links him with education at China Agricultural University full scholarship program at the College of Resources and Environmental Sciences. Now he is a second-year master's student at China Agricultural University and learning different science and technology that China is using for sustainable agricultural production and intensification.

Ibrahim Aliyu Usman

" After all tours in most of the tunnels and rivers across the county, we finally stopped at a STB station which was managed by some CAU students. That demonstrated to us the relevance and importance of drip irrigation and how it encounters water problem in the region. "

Ibrahim Aliyu Usman, 32 years old, worked as an agricultural officer from Federal Ministry of Agriculture and Rural Development Abuja, Nigeria. He studied agricultural extension services from the University of Maiduguri. He is now a member of Sino-Africa STB from the College of Resource and Environmental Science in China Agricultural University at the department of resource utilization and plant protection.

His motto: If you want to go fast, move alone, but if you want to go far, move together.

Aminu Hussaini Adamu

"Thanks to my host and efficient technology of communication and map in China I was able to get to my accommodation a day after my arrival, which was quite an experience and the journey and the destination. That day I met my fellow Nigerians Hamed, who took me to international student building to an eatery for dinner; it's not my first time outside the country and my first to Asia and China."

Aminu Hussaini Adamu was born in Nigeria in the year of 1990 in the city of Kano state in North-West zone of Nigeria. It is in the Sahelian geographic region—South of the Sahara. Kano is the commercial nerve center of Northern Nigeria and the second largest city in Nigeria. He got his first bachelor degree in Kano University of Science and Technology in the year 2009 to 2015 under the Department of Agricultural Economic and Extension (A.E.E). After graduation he started working with Hadejia Ja'amare River Basin Authority as Agric Officer II (Extension Services) on Grade Level 08/2. After he was among the thirty-four African students who got the opportunity to study in China Agricultural University under the program of Science and Technology Backyard (STB). His research title is: Effect of phosphorus containing fertilizer application on yield and growth rate of tomato.

His motto: Never depend on a single income. Make investments to create a second source.

Saturnin Zigani

> **"**I have also learned about soil sampling, yield assessment and the pots experimental activities allowed me to have a mastery about the soil treatment process passing by seed pre-germination, plants' growing parameters measurement to plants maintenance in pots.**"**

From Burkina Faso, aged thirty-five, Saturnin Zigani is an agent of Ministry of Agriculture and Hydro-Development of its country. He has eight years' work experience as an agricultural extension officer. He holds a professional bachelor's degree in plant health risk management from Ouaga II Joseph KY ZERBO University.

Currently, he is in training at the College of Resources and Environmental Sciences, China Agricultural University. He is one of the students of the first promotion of the Sino-African Science and Technology Backyard (STB) project for a Master degree in Resource Utilization and Plant Protection. For this training, he has dedicated himself to millet management and production systems in China. His research topic is "Comparison of millet and soybean intercropping systems response on Nitrogen use efficiency in China and Burkina Faso". His purpose is to learn new techniques, technologies and good agricultural practices in millet management and production that are useful in China and can be adapted to Burkina Faso's condition in order to increase millet yield and contribute to the food security in his country.

His motto: Never give up!

My life in China: a tale of unforgettable experiences

Mudare Shingirai

Back then when I was still a village boy, I had always imagined how it feels to live a different life from the one I had. My name is Mudare Shingirai, a young man aged 29 from Zimbabwe. Currently, I am studying for my master's degree in Resource Utilization, Environmental Science, and Plant Protection at China Agricultural University with the College of Resources and Environmental Sciences. My thoughts and ambitions were always to grow up to be a person with the capacity to change the world that we live in. Seeing my friends and colleagues coming to the village every vacation and going back to their respective schools was one of the things I cherished. More than ever, I became so eager to travel and know as many places as I could. I then promised myself if ever I get the opportunity to explore the world, I would not hesitate. However, the world I imagined at that time was not as diverse as the one I am currently experiencing. Neither did I know that someday I would leave my home country and fly to China, live with the Chinese, and learn a lot from them. I will share my story of how I traveled to China and my greatest experiences so far.

Amazing experiences on the journey to China

After graduating with a bachelor's degree, my ambitions kept pushing me to aim higher. I applied for a Chinese Scholarship Council scholarship and was admitted by China Agricultural University. No one will ever understand the joy that I felt when I got the email from the international office informing me that I had been accepted for the program. From that very point, everything in my life changed. I had spent several sleepless nights, trying to find a way to upgrade and further my education but to no avail. This was the opportunity I had been praying for, and nothing or no one was going to stop me from grabbing it. I started my preparations to travel to China as soon as possible. In my mind, a lot of things were running through my head. I asked myself several questions because I could not believe this was happening. Was I leaving my country, my family, and everyone I knew to go to a place where, among over a billion people, nobody had any idea of who I was?

One thing was certain that I was ready to study and my mind had already been made up. I wanted this so much that even work or leisure was not making sense to me anymore. The thought of flying, airports, everything I had watched on documentaries gave me a thrill that I will never forget. While I was preparing, I started focusing my research more on China: how they live, what they eat, how they relate with foreigners... I found many people giving high rankings to life in China and that made me even hungrier to come. My experience with traveling, let alone by air, was minimal. I had associated with airports only at work, without any intention to travel somewhere. Deep down I would always tell myself that someday I will be the one grabbing my passport, passing through customs, and go. Where would I go? I did not think about it. All I knew was that in the future I was going to fly away. My time to prepare and travel was not that long. I had to deal with a lot of things before I left as I knew my program was going to take more than a year. This meant that I was going to spend a significant part of my life in China.

I paid for my plane ticket in time, as I was advised by the international office. The next step was to visit the Chinese embassy in Harare. There I applied for a student visa, the X1 type. The process was very efficient and I was so grateful when I went to collect my visa. The price, according to me, was also reasonably affordable as compared to other visas. When the day came, I took a bus to OR Tambo international airport from Harare. I then boarded Egypt Air to Cairo. After that, I then took another plane to Beijing. There are times in life you wish you could share your experiences physically with everyone special in your life. Right at that moment when we left Egypt, I wished I could have been with some people to enjoy this experience together.

I arrived in Beijing around 3:00 pm. This was where my unforgettable experience with China began. To begin with, it was the new airport itself, a magnificent piece of world-class engineering. Everything I saw was so amazing: people, the security personnel, the glasswork, floors... I can not mention them all. How the Chinese thought of using self-service machines for checking in is beyond me. With the number of people that I saw flocking into the airport that moment, considering that it was rush hour, I can understand. It was my first time using such a machine that scanned my passport and gave me a receipt. I proceeded to the workers to fill in some details and then went to collect my bag in the baggage area. Beijing international airport is so big!

At this moment, let me mention that some things became so real to me this time. Firstly, the workers spoke their language which is Chinese, which I could not understand. Secondly, I assumed they would understand English. In Zimbabwe our official language is English, therefore I assumed that almost everyone speaks that language. I did not know how misguided I was. Luckily, the international office had provided me with some printed materials so that I would know how I was going to travel when I arrive in Beijing to China Agricultural University, west campus. I was happy at that moment to notice that the Chinese were so loving and happy to see me. Yes, we could not understand each other language-wise, but as humans we did. Some of them took some photos with me. Honestly, I never felt offended, rather I felt so welcome. That was the moment of truth for me, and to some extent, it gave me the confidence that I had lost due to language barriers. One official guided me to a taxi. At the airport there are always taxis ready to transport people to their respective destinations. One can either use a taxi, a subway, or the expressway. People also use buses, but for the fact that I was still new in China, this was not the time to be overconfident.

Arriving at China Agricultural University and experiencing the early life in Beijing

I left the airport in a taxi, meaning in that car there were only two human beings. By the way, we could not have a conversation because of the language barrier. It was then that I thought of checking my cellphone. Wonders never cease to happen. My phone battery had died, and there I was again, stuck in the middle of a new unknown place. I could not let this ruin my moment though, so I decided to look outside my window. What I saw that day was still beyond every word I can use to explain. To begin with, I never imagined people could make things like that so real. China has beautiful roads, bridges, and railway networks. I can not estimate how much time they took to put this into reality, but my wild guess is that this work came from a whole dedicated generation with infinite love for their country.

From the ground up into the skies, all I could see were tall buildings, taller than what I had seen in my country or any neighboring one for that matter. The height is not where the point is, but the fact that most of these buildings are for people to live in! Back at home, we know such developments to be done for businesses, offices, or banks, but here, people live in skyscrapers. Everything is so different, with my experience of each family owning their piece of land and individual house. I had so many questions in my mind how the Chinese got to that stage where they live peacefully in such structures without anyone fighting for individual ownership.

I passed several tollgates, and I noticed that the driver was not using cash to pay for the toll fee. If we had been talking I would have asked, but then I realized that the system is completely automated. Once a car approaches the tollgate, its number is scanned and money is deducted. It began to dawn on me that I had just arrived in an almost cashless society. If someone had cash on them, it would only to be me and a few newcomers. We arrived at China Agricultural University just as the sun began to set. One can just imagine how complicated I thought life was going to be then. Luckily, the university is always alight at night. Electricity never goes out, so the difference between day and night is just barely noticeable. I took out my campus map and started walking down towards the International Students Building. When I arrived, I approached the receptionists and gave them my paperwork. I was the first student from Africa to come for this Science and Technology Backyard. To them, it was pretty straightforward to deal with. We had a few things to settle before they then allowed me to spend the night in what later became my permanent room to this day.

The following morning, I was visited by experts from the department, including Professor Jiao. I was happy to get to meet the people I was here for. A few days passed by and my African colleagues started coming in. We helped each other with the processes such as getting mobile lines, banking, and medical checks. We got to know each other, and to me, it was a happy moment knowing that at least I had people I share something in common with. I then started looking for any colleagues from my country. After some time I got two of them and for the first time, I could speak my local language. That was very important to me, given all the experiences that I had gone through.

After several days of meetings, registrations, and familiarizing myself with the new place, we got along well together. I began to understand the nature of my program with the help from the project assistant Jiangshan. During those days, we also registered with the Department of Exit and Entry before our visas expired. With all these things going on, I had a new experience of using electronic money. Unlike at home where I used several applications for social media, here I began to use WeChat. All the transactions are done on it, while some people prefer to use Alipay. I found WeChat to be a powerful application.

I learned a lot from how convenient online buying was: the availability of raw materials that I could use to make our staple food "Sadza" with either beans, beef, or pork, and a lot of vegetables like tomatoes, cabbage, carrots, etc. While I was doing that, I also learned how to eat with chopsticks. It was such a fascinating experience, given the fact that in my country we normally go naturally with our bare hands. Here and there on special occasions, we make use of forks and knives, but it is rather an imported culture. To this day, I can eat with chopsticks, without any difficulty—what an exciting accomplishment!

The journey to the Great Wall

I had now settled in China, with a renewed mindset, a different perspective of the world altogether. I had associated with many Africans and others from the UK, Pakistan, and Australia. We went to a church called the Beijing International Christian Fellowship. Several Africans meet there on Sundays to practice their faith. It was during these meetings that we organized a visit to the Great Wall.

We left the school by bus with several church members and we had planned to spend a week at a resort near the Great Wall. We started seeing this big wall on our way. In my experience and my wildest dreams, I had never imagined something like that. I mean, how on earth can a human build something so strong yet so long, and yet so high in such difficult mountainous places? Seeing things on television is fine, but the experience of doing it personally is another thing. I am talking about hiking the Great Wall. I was with my countrymate and other church members the day we decided to take the wall. I wore the nice light shoes that I had bought in Beijing, some sweat pants and a long sleeve shirt. I was worried the sun would roast my hands again like it did when I arrived. We were advised to carry a lot of water instead of juices, and something to snack on our way up the wall. So here is the deal. The wall was built to protect the Chinese, historically from conflict. Those who built the wall did not use cement as we do nowadays. They rather used rectangular blocks of rocks. The Great Wall is too long, with official figures around over 21,000 km. We only explored a portion of the wall, and moreover, no one can finish it in a day.

On this day, I was a happy soul, beginning to talk the first step going up the wall. I can not explain the feeling. When you stand below the wall and look back, all you see is the other part going behind and curving into the mountains. With my bag on my side, I took the liberty of taking my first selfie with my phone. Up I went, in a mild rush, taking the rocky steps two at a time. Little did I know that if I proceeded like this I was going to run out of gas before going anywhere. Luckily, we had some individuals who had toured the wall before. They advised us to slow down and check our desires. We wanted to go, as far as the wall could take us. I had not known how long this structure was.

Here and there we would wait for each other and take pictures. By midday, I was beginning to feel my muscles asking me for a break. I sat on a rock of my choice and ate a few chocolates to get more energy. People passed by, and as I re-energized, I could hear others ululating from a distance. The thing with the Great Wall is that the further you go the more you become curious to see more. Also, once there are people ahead of you, they will always make you feel like you can not miss what they are seeing. Yes, and it is that curiosity which then kept me going. After reaching each tower I would pause and take a picture.

This I was going to use to count how many towers I have covered. The Great Wall was built with towers at random spacings. These were used by watchmen to see the enemy from a distance before they attack. Each tower, however, was designed differently: the height of the tower, the windows, and the sizes are some of the things that bring curiosity. You would want to know what the next tower looks like. I hiked until I met my other colleagues and we gathered in a group to take a picture and share some food. Some of us then decided to proceed while others declined. I went further, and the happiest moment of my life at the Great Wall was about to begin. I was hiking and approaching one of the tallest towers from what we had seen at the resort we were staying in. When I arrived, I climbed inside the tower and then realized there was a way up and to the top of the tower. I climbed, there I was, and started whistling and yelling to those who were behind me. The joy that I felt seeing people getting excited coming to the point I was shouting at made me feel like a hero for a moment.

In my mind, I was asking myself if what I saw then was real. I saw several towers behind, each at a distance from each other. I saw the mountains, the green vegetation, the settlements down the mountains, the river flowing, and the people who were fishing. I saw a broken queue of people hiking the Great Wall towards my direction, every one of them sweating and drinking water, washing off their faces, all to see what was beyond the tower!

When the whole crew arrived, we sang little songs, took some pictures, shared some funny stories and some food. To this day, sharing those best moments on the Great Wall has been my greatest experience in China. Thereafter, the sun was about to set. We then began descending the wall to arrive in time for dinner. Well, in my opinion, hiking the Great Wall might have been difficult, with a lot of thirsts, sweat, brushes from trees and rocks, but nothing beats using your whole body to brace yourself when you are going down the wall. I have to say that this part might be more exhausting than going up. And, if one is not so careful with what they step on, the probabilities of falling are extremely high. Occasionally I would take pictures on our way down.

My bag was now lighter, with all the water and food finished. We made it to the guest house at around 5:00 pm. Straightway I jumped into the cool shower before I put on some clean clothes. I joined other colleagues at the dinner table. I could tell that everyone had a story to tell, the excitement in the room, and how I felt it was almost tangible. However, the muscles would not let us get away with it, and everyone had to retire to their rooms and sleep. That night, I think I had the deepest sleep I had ever done in my life.

Traveling to Quzhou Experimental Station

We, as master students from the School of Environmental Science and Plant Protection, left China Agricultural University to conduct field trials in Quzhou County, Hebei. This was part of the requirements of the program such that African students learn from the Chinese experts on knowledge transfer to the farmers. Through the leadership of Professor Jiao Xiaoqiang, we checked out of the dormitory following the university regulations. All students and staff were given protective utilities such as masks and sanitizers before leaving the campus with the school bus. The journey was fascinating as it was an opportunity to see the outside world, that is out of Beijing. As the traveling continued, I witnessed commercial agriculture, particularly in wheat (*Triticum aestivum*) and peaches (*Prunus persica*).

Most of the wheat crops exhibited signs of physiological maturity. By visually observing through the window I could tell the peach fruits were ready for consumption. The vegetation on the side of the roads, the mountains together with properly paved roads made the journey more memorable. Upon arrival, students met with the leadership of the Quzhou Experimental Station, Professor Rongfeng. From there, the students checked in with the local police, with the assistance of Professor Jiao. The police took some photos with individual students holding their passports. We were allocated our rooms, which were already prepared with blankets, chairs, electricity, running water, and other necessary items. Dinner was served in the restaurant at around 7:00 pm and most of the students enjoyed it. After dinner, a welcome meeting was held later at 8:00 pm. Professor Jiao Xiaoqiang, Professor Jiang Rongfeng and other staff were present for the short briefings. Students were given instructions on the program for the following day. We were strongly advised to communicate with their Chinese partners who were already in Quzhou by Professor Jiao.

He further went on highlighting other key aspects of project proposals, meta-analysis, and literature review. A brief background about Quzhou and the importance of the station as well as the background on soil fertility issues which gave rise to the need for intensive research on this location was described by Prof Rongfeng. Thereafter, students were allowed to ask questions. From the initial day, it was interesting to arrive and see how much the university had made the place conducive for learning. It was indeed a great success for students to be at Quzhou Experimental Station since it has experts with vast experiences in working with farmers, research, and training students.

Experiences from Wanzhuang STB village

We visited a Science and Technology Backyard known as Wanzhaung on several occasions to learn various practical experiences from farmers. The farmers grow wheat with assistance from students and lecturers from China Agricultural University. In the field, I had the opportunity to interact with several experts. I learned a lot about wheat agronomy, from planting, fertilizer management, irrigation, and the major summer maize winter wheat rotation system. The farmers grew a high yielding wheat variety that is known to be rich in protein. The wheat rows are structured in such a way that they leave space about 15cm to plant the following maize crop. The crop was at the physiological maturity stage. Harvesting was done mechanically with a combine harvester.

The activities were interesting since I participated in the collection of grain and yield estimations. Almost all sections during the harvesting were captured with a drone mounted with a camera. Important to note is that this mechanization process involves the use of GPS for precision. Later on, after the summer maize season, I visited the village for the harvesting of maize. I worked together with some Chinese students to calculate yield-related parameters. This was a great opportunity for me to exchange knowledge with my Chinese counterparts.

Irrigation and water resource management in Quzhou county

We visited various farmers in Quzhou county to study irrigation management. Just close to the experimental station, we stopped a few kilometers to see farmers who were using their water pumps to irrigate various crops. According to Professor Zhang Hongyan, irrigation further away from the main river was more expensive than for those who stayed close to the water source. It cost around 20 RMB to irrigate four times a day. These farmers, as I noticed, practiced different kinds of intercropping. Notably, throughout the journey, I saw tree-cotton, tree-stevia-groundnuts, tree-sunflower, and tree-stevia-sweet potato cropping systems. It was also easy to see a lot of wheat fields and a reasonable area of maize. Most of the wheat had already been harvested, by combine and manually for those with difficult land areas.

Farmers in Quzhou access water from tunnels that have been connected to the Fuyang river. It is on this river that most of them around the experimental station survive. However, in other areas, farmers use deep good irrigation. As a result, the electricity to draw the water from underneath is expensive, hence the cost of production. What I was happy about is that both farmers, far or closer to the water sources, were still exceptionally organized. The level of coordination and understanding by the farmers was very commendable. The other important factor that the teacher explained was the cost of installing boreholes. Not all farmers can afford it and a few of them resort to shallow-well irrigation. The Chinese government had played a role in installing irrigation equipment for its people. It is this move that has made a milestone impact on agriculture productivity in China.

I also had the opportunity to witness the major problems China is facing in its agriculture sector. As I was traveling and observing, I noticed how bad the soil has been degraded and the cracks that were on the surfaces. I also saw farmers struggling with wheat straw when they were planting maize. Furthermore, I realized how difficult it was with the water situation, which was the reason why China has even resorted to constructing man-made rivers. The water in the rivers was also not very clean and potable as I had expected.

On a much positive note, I was impressed by the intensive horticulture in and out of the greenhouses. I had the feeling that Chinese farmers were dedicated when it comes to their food production.

Mechanical millet planting at Quzhou Experimental Station

My knowledge of millet production was not as vast as that of maize, since the latter forms the staple food in Zimbabwe. One day I joined my Chinese colleague Peng Pu, two Chinese farmers, and a tractor driver to plant millet. Zheng 16 and Zheng 18 were used for the field experiment. Planting was done following a previous mung bean crop that we had recently harvested.

Basal fertilizer was applied together with the millet seeds in both the whole-farm mechanization experiment and the millet mung bean rotation experiment. Since the planter that was used was specifically for millet, we could not plant maize in our plots. Arrangements were underway to carry out the activity within a few days. During the exercise, I was overjoyed to take part in driving the tractor while planting millet.

The project proposal defense day

After a long period of preparations and exhaustive work, the day had arrived. Proposals defending had started the day before, and some of my colleagues and I were scheduled to be the last presenters. This was my first time to do a presentation with panelists in different locations. At Quzhou Experimental Station we were led by Professor Jiao Xiaoqiang, Professor Zhang Hongyan, and Professor Jiang Rongfeng. There were other assessors online, and the committee from my college. My supervisor, Dr. Cong Wenfeng was the chairman of today's activity. Several colleagues presented before me in the morning. After the tea break, I then presented and received some comments and contributions from the committee. Overall, every student got assistance from all panelists depending on his or her topic.

Furthermore, having time to interact with other experts as well as my supervisor gave me a good impression. Some of my colleagues were presenting from Africa while others were in Beijing. Those in Beijing had an advantage since connectivity was better. However, the African counterparts did struggle with the internet to the extent that we had to improvise and make sure they completed their task. At the end of the session, overall suggestions were given by the chairman of the committee, and a group photo was taken for students in Quzhou with the professors. Professor Jiao then mentioned that we would meet in the evening for a discussion about how to incorporate the suggestions from the panelists into our work. I applauded the perseverance that he had to see us produce better results as each day passed.

Visiting Dezhong STB

I reinforced the knowledge on grape production that I gained before, the problems associated, and the major roles being played by the Chinese STB students. Unlike my previous experience in Qianya village, the visit to Dezhong STB was different because the grape production was mainly done in greenhouses. They produced at least five types of grapes, all of which can be consumed fresh or processed into wine. We had the opportunity to test these products, while one of the STB students took us through the details of this place. Dezhong STB was founded due to more or less the same problems that the other villages were facing which include poor soil fertility management, poor irrigation, pests and diseases, and low market value for grape yields. When the STB was created, they started by surveying the area and experimenting to test various production factors. The key to the observations was that the soil pH was too high, ranging to about eight, which is not recommended for optimum crop growth. They then introduced several technologies including remote sensing for diseases, humidity, and temperature in the greenhouses. A lot of progress was made in terms of yield and quality of grapes, with increases in overall revenue. However, the quality of the soil still needed a lot of attention, as it was prone to cracking. Hopefully, with the guidance of experts from the university and students, the farmers now have a better understanding of farming in a much sustainable way.

Post-harvest management of maize in Quzhou county

Once the maize has been harvested from the farmers' fields, the farmers ensure that the maize needs to be dried up. There is not enough space in China. Therefore, farmers have a challenge in managing yields. As a result, farmers put their maize in different places, such as on the rooftops and by the roadside. Once the maize is dry, there is coordinated shelling of the cobs. I have been observing this phenomenon in Quzhou county. It took about four people to complete the task of shelling. Two people used large shovels to get the maize in a somewhat linear heap. A machine then came in, which has been designed to pick cobs with its front rim. The rim was connected to a conveyor belt which brought the cobs to the sheller. The sheller then separated the grains from the cobs.

Later on, the grains were sieved and exited through another opening. The crushed cobs were then dropped to another side. Even though this whole activity was done on the floor, there was still an opportunity to let the grains stay for further drying. Most importantly, the process was much faster as compared to the African way of shelling using bare hands.

Apple production in Quzhou county

I visited one of the STB villages to learn in practice about the production of apples in China. We were led by Prof. Zhang Hongyan and Prof. Jiang Rongfeng. They explained to us that this region was generally not specific for apple production. However, because farmers who grow other crops such as maize want to increase income, they set aside land for producing apples. This move has seen farmers improve in their livelihoods since the apples started bearing fruits. In the orchard, activities such as manuring for nutrient addition, mulching to improve water conservation, pruning, and trimming to manage plant density are done. Below the apple trees, one can see plastics that are used to reflect light. This technique helps to increases sugars in the apples. The fruits themselves are bagged in plastic pockets to protect them from insects and dust.

Chinese farmers use simple tractors, planters, and other innovative tools to make the working very easy for them. My other greatest pleasure was seeing the use of drone technology to film real-time farming events and also spraying chemical pesticides. In other parts, the drones are used for sowing trees in mountainous areas that would not be accessible by humans.

In my view, the Science and Technology Backyard model is a very big strategy that Africa can adopt to improve food security. The desire is still up to this day for me to go back to the village and spend time with the Chinese farmers. They are loving people, with a lot of wisdom and experience. They are hardworking, focused, and very time conscious.

Above all, I will never forget that they treated us with a lot of respect and they were also willing to learn from us. We exchanged a lot of things, such as stories and moments, and I learned a lot about cultural differences. In every experience I got from the county I would also want to acknowledge the student-teacher relationship of mine that improved as I stayed at Quzhou Experimental Station. We had experts like Professor Rongfeng, Professor Hongyan, and Professor Xiaoqiang. Several other professors would occasionally come to the station and share their expertise with us and return to Beijing. Quzhou will always be at my heart because it was the first place for me to do an online presentation and hold classes online. I will never forget this great experience in my lifetime. In conclusion, my experience in China has offered me several opportunities I shall cherish as I explore the world.

Living my dreams in China

Amani Stephen Milinga

I arrived in Beijing, China in mid-September of 2019 from Tanzania. I was excited as I was going to start a new life in a foreign country. Joining China Agricultural University promised to be a golden opportunity to receive training from world class professors and in an international environment. Also I saw it as an opportunity to meet people from different academic and cultural backgrounds and therefore learn from each other. Landed in Beijing Capital International Airport around 00:15 mid night and followed landing formalities, as a foreigner I thought it was not a good idea to move to the campus that night so I decided to wait around the airport area until sunrise. Luckily enough, in the morning I met a fellow Tanzanian who spoke Chinese and helped me to get a ride to our campus in Haidian district.

In the first few weeks, communication was so hard, as many people around public places such as subway stations, shopping malls, hospitals, and even around campus hardly speak English.

Our academic course started around 11th of October, soon after the National Day holiday. And our first class was Chinese language which I think was very interesting as I was eager to learn a new language especially Mandarin. Other courses involve organic farming, agricultural non-point pollution, integrated management of pest and diseases, research and academic norms, thesis writing in plant nutrition, advanced experimental designs, etc.

We finished our first semester in mid-January. Many thanks to the Chinese government for their all-out war against the pandemic and taking care of us all the time and providing all support needed to sustain our stay in China.

I almost spent my entire Spring Festival around the campus. After a prolonged lockdown, we finally made our way to Quzhou, Hebei province, for practical education.

A trip to Hebei

I started the day by travelling from Beijing, the Capital of China, and heading directly to Hebei province and finally reporting to the Quzhou Experiment Station which is operated by China Agricultural University.

The trip itself has been convenient as we took a rental bus service which was organized by our college.

I have learned when this station was established, and hence why we are here as an African student combined with Chinese students to stay for a couple of months in this station to learn how to conduct field trials and most importantly, how to communicate with farmers about the outcome of our experiment. I came to realize that China has invested hugely in the agricultural research so as to come up with solutions for the real challenges facing smallholders' farmers and agriculture as a sector. I have also learned that, if the younger generation like us will be exposed to the high agricultural training like this one, it will attract and motivate more and more young people to participate in agricultural area of expertise and agriculture chain of production.

I have also learned that everything to be successful in life, everything should be well prepared. Talking about the way the trip was organized, the reception and the facilities around the station told me that this project was meant to be one of the most successful projects in agriculture between China and Africa. I also learned that China as a country has achieved food security thanks to joint efforts among agriculture and related sectors to achieve the common goal.

This is the big lesson and motivation for me to try my best to shape myself in a way that will make me more fruitful and hence contribute to the intensification of agriculture back home. Also, the fact that this project draws attention from other reputable stakeholders like Food and Agriculture Organization of the United Nations (FAO), Warner Bros (WB), Bill and Melinda Gates Foundation teaches me the importance of global partnership to fight against hunger.

Tonight, as I sit down to write this summary of these days, I honestly feel motivated, cared for, and well prepared to pursue this noble course of humanity—food security. As one wise man once said "Everything can wait, except Agriculture", I will go back to Africa and push the agricultural transformation across the continent and maintain a good relationship between China and Africa in the field of Agriculture.

I would like to pinpoint out my expectations that in the next few months I would like to be actively engaged in this training program, working together with teachers, staff and Chinese students so that we can learn from each other and maintain lifelong relationship.

Trip to irrigation management station

Today is June 10, 2020, I have two major activities. One is to visit some fields to learn about irrigation water management technologies and the other is to work on long-term winter-wheat summer-maize experiment located at 300 mu (a unit of area measurement commonly used in China).

The first stop was at the river irrigation technology

At this field we learned how farmers who have a field near the river can take advantage of irrigating their crops by pumping water from the nearby river and directing it to the field using plastic pipes. This method is cheap and convenient for the farmers who cultivate near the river. Also I had special experience seeing farmers plant trees along the river to protect the environment and ecosystems as well as building the network of forests.

The second stop was at the network of river irrigation

At this point we experienced how farmers together with village leaders organized the network of man-made rivers so as to get water to irrigate their crops and finally secure food security. This network of rivers fetches water from the Yellow River so farmers manage the water according to their needs and seasons.

The third stop was at the well irrigation technology

This technology is specifically for the farmers that have fields far away from the river. They dig a well and pump underground water using electricity and apply the water to the crop. In my view, this technology is very good for the African farmers especially for the farmers away from the rivers or fresh water lakes.

The last stop was at the drip irrigation technology

At this station, two CAU students worked together with farmers and the local community to demonstrate the drip irrigation in grapes. Farmers in this village use flooding irrigation which loses a lot of water due to evaporation, leaching and untargeted application of water. This also causes a lot of energy resources loss which increases production costs.

Drip irrigation technology will save a lot of water and thereby energy. Also drip irrigation technology provides a chance to apply water and fertilizer at the same time when the fertilizer is dissolved into water before being directed to the farm. This technology will save a lot of time and energy. However, a lot of studies are needed especially for African smallholders to apply this technology.

Working at long-term winter-wheat summer-maize crop rotation system experiment

I went to work at 300 mu field where long-term experiment is carried out on winter-wheat summer-maize cropping system.

We supervised maize planting and also we were placing plastic pegs on the plots to mark the field plots.

The proposal defense of Sino-Africa STB master students

June 26, 2020, I had breakfast at our canteen at 07:30 am and then headed to the classroom to attend the proposal defense of Sino-African STB master students. A total number of 15 master's students presented our research proposal today. We received comments, suggestions and questions from the evaluation committee. On my part, I presented my research on the influence of tillage, straws and nitrogen in maize production in North China Plains.

After presentation I received two comments from the evaluation committee with regard to my research on maize.

One comment was about to do the experiment in two seasons – this will be discussed with my supervisor to see the possibility of doing two seasons as it is practically possible.

The second suggestion was to compare the data from 10 previous years since this is a long term experiment. I honestly agree with the suggestions and comments from the evaluation team.

Maize growth monitoring

Our main activity was to measure growth parameters: plant height, plant girth, leaf area index, number of old leaf and number of young leaf.

We started to work by selecting randomly three plants from each plot and measuring appropriate growth parameters.

Ⅰ. Plant height—was measured using tape measure by fixing the tape at the ground surface and extending it to the tip of the maize plant. Appropriate height was recorded in the notebook.

Ⅱ. Plant girth—was measured using the tape measure by surrounding it around the bottom of the maize plant and girth was recorded in the notebook.

Ⅲ. Leaf area index (LAI)—was recorded by measuring the length and width of the first three leaves from the bottom by using a tape measure and recorded in the notebook.

Ⅳ. Numbers of leaf (old and young leaf)—were physically counted and recorded in the notebook.

Among the total of 54 plots of the experiment we managed to visit 27 plots, and returned to the research station.

These parameters will be used to assess how tillage, straws and nitrogen can affect the maize plant growth.

Dezhong STB visit

This STB is involved in producing grapes as a major crop. Other crops include maize, cucumber, pumpkin and sunflower. Dezhong STB was established in April 2018 and is located at Quzhou town, Quzhou county in Hebei and the responsible teachers are Professor Li Xiaolin, Professor Zhang Weifeng, Professor Zhang Hongyan and Teacher Wang Shaolei.

The STB was established with the goal of green production and industrial prosperity, and it is the driving force for the development. We learned about production constraints which led to the establishment of this STB which include the poor soil fertility management in grapes production.

Farmers' survey

I went out of the station to help my Chinese partner with farmers' survey. We visited two villages and interviewed four farmers: two from Wangzhuang village and the other two from Matuan village.

The aim of the farmers' survey was to identify farmers who practice maize-winter wheat cropping rotation in the Quzhou area.

International Food Day: Food Security Public Awareness

On October 16, 2020, I went to participate in commemorating the International Food Day in the Quzhou Experimental Station. There was a public awareness campaign about food security for primary and middle school students in which more than 1,000 students participated. International Food Day is observed by all member states of the United Nations.

Field observation meeting at Xianggongzhuang

On October 21, 2020, we started a trip to Xianggongzhuang village to participate in the field observation meeting.

Xianggongzhuang village has held an Apple Science and Technology Backyard from 2010. Before this STB, farmers only planted food crops such as maize and wheat in rotation. But to unleash their economic potential, these farmers decided to shift over to starting apple orchards with more than 15 different varieties. These apples are produced during summer using green technology so chemical input is substantially reduced.

Fertilizers used are manure from pigs and chickens, pest and diseases are controlled culturally and mechanically by using pest and insects traps. Soil is covered with live mulch such as green grass, and apple ridges are covered with plastic to increase light intensity to give apples more reddish color.

Friendship visit at Situan Middle School

We started a trip to the nearby Situan Middle School to give the interesting English oral classes to the young students. We arrived at school and were welcomed by teachers and students and thereafter we divided ourselves into groups of two members and started to give oral classes to the young students.

After oral classes we went to the playgrounds where we sang some interesting songs and then played football.

Maize threshing and measurement

On October 28, 2020, I went to the self-study room to analyze data collected from my experimental plots. I was analyzing data with regard to SPAD whereby I was calculating the average SPAD from each of the three maize plants so as to get the SPAD of the plot.

In the afternoon, my friends Solomon, Li Yiming and I went to the laboratory to thresh maize cobs which had been oven-dried.

Maize samples for long term experiment A, B and C were measured for whole maize grain, and then the weight without stover was also measured.

At 4:00 pm we received some news reporters from Hebei TV who interviewed us about the general activities and our working relationship with Chinese counterparts.

Finally, we finished our stay in Quzhou and returned to Beijing to continue with studies and further our education. I would like to say that my one year in China has been so life-changing because I have learned a lot and exchanged culture with Chinese and other international friends, teachers and students.

My journey to delightful life and hands-on learning in China

Bilisuma Kabeto Wako

On September 10, 2019, my friend and I landed on the land of China. It was a very difficult journey because of very long distance and we used transit line to come to China and it was midnight when we landed. We stayed in the airport for more than five hours. In the early morning of September 11, 2019, we went out of the airport, took a taxi to the west campus of China Agricultural University. Both of us were very tired and didn't even talk to each other, because we hadn't slept for two days. After thirty minutes we arrived at the campus and got into our accommodation. After that we took a rest, arranged our belongings in shelf and started to communicate with students who came before us about the registration and some other things to be done. Things were totally different compared to our country Ethiopia. The food, the weather, the language… everything was very difficult at that time. After struggling to deal with those things, I finally adapted to the new environment and started to live a normal life. After some time we did registration and started to select courses for the first semester of 2019. It was a really difficult task because everything was put into the system in Chinese characters, as a result we couldn't do anything but ask for help even for very simple questions. There were eight courses of the first semester: elementary Chinese, organic farming, efficient utilization of agro produce, nonpoint source pollution of agriculture, thesis writing, biometrics and experimental design, rural revitalization and innovation and research integrity and academic norms. These courses were managed by one professor, but taught by different professors from the same university/college and different companies. The course was also supported by excursion which made our learning process more fruitful. It was very interesting and joyful study time.

Meta-analysis and thesis

According to the discussion with my supervisor, I was going to conduct a meta-analysis on the effect of chemical phosphorus fertilizer on maize yield in Africa and China. It will be conducted in three parts. The first part was meta-analysis of the effect of chemical P fertilizer in Africa and China. The second is the field experiment in China and the third is farm survey in Ethiopia. On May 1, 2020, I was told to submit on each day the extracts of necessary data of a minimum of five papers from peer-reviewed journals conducted in different parts of Africa on the aforementioned topic. During our discussion, my supervisor assigned one Chinese Ph.D student to help me through the process of doing meta-analysis. It was a really difficult and timeconsuming task that I was given—we didn't even have enough time to search for and extract data from five papers. It was during this time that I slept the shortest time in my studies in China. I collected papers starting early morning to around 4:00 pm, and in the afternoon, I extracted the data and started to fill in the data sheet. After submitting it in the night at around 10:00 pm, I started to look for articles again, because it was very difficult to find the right papers that meet the required criteria. It took me almost one month to almost complete the number of observations required—that was a minimum of 2,000 observations from Africa.

Journey to Quzhou Experimental Station

On June 2, 2020 the program coordinator arranged internship at Quzhou Experimental Station in Hebei province. Following this schedule, we started our journey to Quzhou Experimental Station. Here are some points that I remember on my way to Quzhou. In the early morning all students prepared their baggages and got ready for the journey. The bus arrived, the baggages were loaded, for all students face masks were distributed as a safety measure against Covid -19, and lastly whether all students were onboard was checked and then the journey was formally started. As soon as the journey started, orientation was given on what to do, when to do, with whom to do and how to do by Professor Jiao Xiaoqiang (STB project coordinator). The journey was very interesting because Chinese rural environment was new to all students and due to lockdown of Covid-19 we had not been exposed to outside campus for almost five months, but then we were looking at the scenery of the China rural environments, the crops and infrastructures. On our way to Quzhou we took a rest for 30 minutes, bought some food and vegetables and enjoyed. After travelling almost for five hours we finally arrived at Quzhou Experimental

Station. Then as soon as we arrived at the experimental station, the welcoming address was given by the professors and Chinese students and we were given again some safety equipments like masks and tissue papers. We were finally taken to the rooms prepared for us. In this part of our journey, what I didn't really hesitate to appreciate was the hospitality of STB staff. Before arriving there, everyone assumed the station is not conducive for living, but after we had arrived there, it was totally different from our expectation that the Quzhou Experiment Station is beautiful with conducive environment.

Farmers' field school in Quzhou

The second and most important event organized by the Chinese STB students and farmers on June 2, 2020 was to visit the farmers field school 4-5km away from the Quzhou Experiment Station. I, together with some of my friends, joined our professor to the visit. I really appreciate the farmers' hospitality; I feel really proud to be part of STB. Even though it was organized in Chinese language, I learned a lot from them. All local communities took part and showed us their respect and the technologies that China Agricultural University is working with them collaboratively. I also learned that, students doing their master thesis or Ph.D present what they did and discuss the results with farmers—this is a huge input for agricultural development and technology transfer. Finally, we visited a field with sativa crop. This was my first time to hear and learn about this crop. It was a really inspiring cash crop that is used as a substitute for sugar and used as tea. It is the healthiest crop with less glucose to replace sugar. Another very important thing I learned was how farmers are adjusting the temperature for the crop. They cover them with plastic during the cold season to increase and optimize temperature, and after season changes and temperature increases, they again cover with soil to adjust temperature for the root. Even though it is labor-intensive, it is a very interesting practice.

Cooking in Quzhou Experimental Station

The Quzhou Experimental Station prepared a kitchen for us and I started to cook food in Quzhou which I was not doing in Beijing. It was very interesting to cook and eat my favorite food of my own choice. Fruit and vegetables and other commodities were at affordable price in Quzhou and I really enjoyed everything from a life perspective. The kitchen was initially prepared for only Muslim students, however since most students were interested in cooking, we discussed with our coordinators who allowed us to cook. Initially it was very interesting that we cooked together and ate together, but at last we started to cook separately because everyone of us focused on our practical learning and planned our time of eating and cooking individually.

My practical learning in Quzhou Experimental Station

I did four main basic tasks in Quzhou Experimental Station. The first was pot experiment on the effect of different levels of P supply intensity on maize root and shoot biomass. This was done in collaboration with Chinese partner Gong Haiqing. It was really difficult and time-consuming. We prepared plastic bags, measured fertilizer, and mix fertilizer with soil, sieve soil to remove some big particles, and plant maize finally. Generally, what I did and learned in Quzhou Experimental Station is summarized as follows.

The first and most important thing was field experiment in Quzhou Experimental Station. It was conducted to identify the effect of chemical P fertilizer on maize shoot and root biomass at different growth stages of maize. The maize was planted ten days after the first batch was planted on July 6, 2020 untill the final batch was planted on September 21, 2020. Through this long time all activities conducted including land preparation, planting, weeding, watering and monitoring and evaluation of the field, all done jointly with supervisors and Chinese partners. The achievement from this practical experimental learning was considerable agronomic practice of maize and the effect of chemical P fertilizer on maize shoot and root biomass. I strongly believe that practical learning would help me realizing the good agronomic practice of maize back in my home country after obtaining my degree, and help me in assisting small holder's subsistence farmers to realize their food self-sufficiency. The major indicators measured were: shoot biomass, root biomass, root length, plant height, leaf number per plant, number of lateral roots, and leaf area. The result indicated significant difference between two treatments favoring the importance of P fertilizer on maize shoot and root at different growth stages. Knowing this effect at different growth stages will help to effectively manage P fertilizer to achieve high efficiency and high production as well as reducing detrimental effect of P fertilizer on environmental safety. Based on this practical learning and my achievement from it, I will develop the basic P fertilizer application methods and procedure that will improve the production and productivity of maize focusing on small holder farmers in developing countries.

The second and most important part was greenhouse pot experiment on the effect of different supply intensity of P fertilizer on maize root and shoot. The activity was designed to know the effect of different levels of P supply (i.e. 200mg/kg and 400mg/kg) on maize shoot and root. It was designed to be sampled two times, that were at V6 and V12 the stages of maize growth. I used a plastic pot with the size of 50cm height and 40cm diameter. From beginning of pot preparation to final harvesting of the experiment I jointly did with my supervisors and Chinese partners. In collaboration with them I learned different procedures of work that build my knowledge base. It was planted on June 13, 2020. Then I started to manage the experiment according to the water requirement of the maize every day and after one week of planting I started to take data of plant height and leaf number. The leaves number data taken were divided into expanded and unexpanded leaves. At V6 stage, I harvested half of the plants to see the effect at this growth stage of maize. The parameters measured were: plant height, leaf number, root length, shoot biomass, root biomass, leaf area, SPAD value (chlorophyll content), and root angle and P uptake and P concentration in the shoot part of maize. The result indicated significant difference between different groups of P supply intensity. According to the practical learning/experiment result, the treatment with P 200mg/kg of soil showed significantly higher values of all the measured parameters. This was very impressive result indicating that as the level of P fertilizer application increases, maize shoot and root components will not increase in corresponding ratio. For example, the root biomass of P 200mg/kg treatments was significantly higher manifesting a good nutrient absorption from the soil and good plant performance than two level of treatments. After taking sample at V6 stage I continued managing half of experiment which was left to be harvested at V12 stage. I harvested all the treatment when they reached V12 stage and all the parameters that were measured at V6 were measured again to see the effect of P fertilizer at different growth stage with different P supply. At this stage also the experiment manifested the optimum P fertilizer supply was 200mg/kg. What I learned from this experiment was very impressive and it is a base for agronomic skill that I need to help farmers after graduation. This can be categorized into two: the first one is P fertilizer is very important for maize growth as indicated by the experimental learning, treatments with no P fertilizer were significantly less than the other two treatments in all parameter measured. The second point is as the level of P fertilizer application increases, there is no corresponding increase of maize shoot and root components which was identified by the difference between 200mg/kg and 400mg/kg of the maize at V6 and V12 stage. Even though some results indicate more value for higher P fertilizer application, it was not economical and profitable to apply more P fertilizer and my conclusion from this experimental learning was the optimum

P fertilizer should have to be applied to achieve high yield and highly efficient maize yield. Generally, this part of my stay in Quzhou Experimental Station was fundamental and I learned a lot from it.

Collaborative work for my practical learning in Quzhou Experimental Station

To support my practical learning, I conducted the experiments with Chinese friends on the effect of different types of P fertilizer at the same P supply intensity of 150mg/kg on two types of soils (acidic and calcareous). It was through this experimental learning that I acquired the basic agronomic practice of maize cultivation in China. To enhance my practical learning, I had also been involved in every activity performed on the long-term field experiment conducted by my Chinese partner on different levels of P supply to maize production. Sample taking, root scanning, measuring plant height and leaf areas, and crushing the sample of shoot to identify nutrient content were the major activities undertaken in collaboration with my Chinese friend. Through this process, valuable knowledge and skill were gained, which deepened my understanding of the agronomic practice of maize.

Visitation to different STBs in Quzhou county

The third part of my practical learning was the practical visitation to STBs and experiencing a good technology that farmers, agricultural cooperatives and companies are practicing in different Science and Technology Backyards (STBs) located in Quzhou county, Hebei province. There were different STBs that I had visited and acquire some very important knowledge on how science and technology backyards work with the farmers. Among them, Wangzhuang STB was a wonderful one. In this STB a group of scientists, university professors, students, farmers and village leaders sat together, discussed the problems of agricultural production, provided possible solutions together and finally implemented the suggested solutions together. Through this mechanism the STB solved the bottle necks of agricultural production in the village and transformed the village into a successful model village in agricultural production. One of the most impressive things I learned from this STB was the clustering of village into one technology model. Through this clustering method, they solved the problem of land fragmentation by creating a large farm that can be easily mechanized. The farmers do everything together but harvest from their land, making it very suitable for agricultural mechanization. I had visited other STBs established on specific commodities like apple and grape as well as other agricultural companies operating on different agricultural technologies. Beside STBs and companies, I had learned a lot through visiting different irrigation systems that farmers were using in the Quzhou county and how Chinese government managed water resource through diverting water from water sufficient areas to water scare areas, making water available for irrigation.

More importantly I am really impressed by how scientists solved the problem of water salinity used for irrigation by investigating over time and recommending a deep well rather than shallow well and totally eliminating salinity through a time. For example, on August 25, 2020 we African STB students went to Baizhai STB. On that occasion the village head and Chinese students who worked there gave awareness about the improved and the already available varieties to the local community and scientific communities which included students and university professors. After brief introduction, farmers and other stakeholders selected varieties based on different criteria of their choice, and finally a lot of media briefings were made and group photo was taken and we headed to the grape farm. At the grape farm we learned how they produced the grape and discussed how it would be propagated for multiplication. The other example was on June 10, 2020 from visitation of water and irrigation system in China. We started our visit to farmers field with pepper, beans and trees intercropped. Farmers used nearby water source which is cheap and easy to irrigate their farm. Then we headed to another place looking at the greenery and scenic farmers through the glass of the bus. Professor. Hongyan Zhang gave us a brief description of how farmers use river for irrigation. After that we headed to another place with a beautiful bridge made of timber wood and some strong wire and it is really amazing. Here we visited a maize, eggplant and cabbage field on which the performance of each crop is very good. After that we arrived at a place called Huangkou water gate. In this place, water comes from different sources like man-made sources of water and the water from big reservoir from mountain areas. The water is controlled by the water gate and diverted in man-made channel and then divided into different small channels and then reach fields for irrigation. The water is transported from the South China to North China because China has engineers in water transporting, as a result water from Yellow River and Yangtze River can be used in other places for irrigation. The water is managed in the manner that it is not on one side only, it is adjusted through the water gate. A few minutes later, we arrived at a place called Beiyou, the place where the first STB was established eleven years ago. At this site we learned how farmers use irrigation water from the well, and how farmers planted the maize on the straw of wheat. Prof. Hongyan Zhang described the importance of wheat straw as it minimizes water evaporation and improves soil organic matter. Finally we visited a grape producing village in which farmers use traditional way of irrigation and consuming water resources. Two CAU students working on how to efficiently use water for irrigation and fertilizer gave us a brief description of what they were doing. Generally, in this part I learned very important agricultural technologies that improved my understanding of science and technology in China and helped me in my future career to transform agricultural sector to the best of my knowledge I gained here.

Another important thing was daily report during my practical learning: this is comprehensive reporting of what I did each day since I started practical learning in Quzhou Experimental Station. Recording and reporting every day, what I did gave me considerable hint on how to organize things in a good manner. Through this process a good and comprehensive mechanism of monitoring and evaluation was developed between me and my supervisor— discussing the knowledge gained and the problem encountered on my practical learning with suggested solution was very imperative tool of learning. I wrote a total of 131 daily reports of what I practically learned in Quzhou Experimental Station. In Quzhou Experimental Station I stayed and got considerable, inclusive and comprehensive understanding of things which cover practical learning skills on basic agronomy of maize, focusing on P fertilizer management, Science and Technology Backyard community mobilization through agricultural technologies and comprehensive quality improvement on organizing and managing things.

Coming back to Beijing from Quzhou Experimental Station

At the end, when we were ready to come back to Beijing together with all students and some professors from international students' office and project coordinators, a joint memory of what we did in Quzhou Experimental Station was done through organizing media. We went to farmers' house and discussed with them some important events of their daily life. And also, we visited their farms. And finally, the program coordinators arranged a farewell party in the evening together with dinner which we enjoyed a lot. In the morning, when we were about to leave the experimental station, together with all the staff of

Quzhou Experimental Station and some professors we took group photos in four places. The first place was in front of the international cooperation center building, the second was in front of the green house, the third was in front of the administration building and finally at the gate of the experimental station.

Then, we said goodbye to Quzhou and started our journey back to Beijing, China Agricultural University. On the way, it was very interesting to look at the beautiful scenery from the window of the bus in different rural and small cities of China. It was only one stop for a restroom and to buy things for only five minutes. The most difficult part was when we were about to enter Beijing city. Due to Covid-19 inward movement restrictions, police checked the security of all students and then we stayed more than two hours to get permission to enter Beijing. After getting permission we started the journey again and reached our destination at 10:00 pm.

Finally, I started to analyze the data of the pot and field experiments that were done in Quzhou, through discussion with my supervisor.

Working Experience in China

Buana Suefo

My dream: To study in China and focus on transforming agriculture in Africa

China is currently the fastest growing country in the world. It has made an effort to provide scholarships to foreigners, thus contributing significantly to the technical training of several global level citizens. So, looking at this huge advantage, I applied to study in China. It has always a dream since childhood to enjoy this beautiful country. Whenever I buy something, it is said that it was made in China, so the curiosity of one day to visit it was extremely strong.

Welcome to China

On September 11, I finished the registration process in the international office. There was a meeting to give welcoming notes to all international students, a ceremony that was led by the Vice President of the CAU who very briefly introduced the functioning of the university, regulations and general rules of governance and also illustrated the map of the city, as well as the sanctions carried out for academia fraud as a general functioning of the academy.

After that meeting, I had another meeting which explained the functioning of the STB programme, which was chaired by Professor Xiaoqiang Jiao and attended by several participants and/or actors involved in the project such as the representative of the World Bank, etc.

Then, after these introductory notes, we started the Elementary Chinese course and other courses: Efficient Utilization of Agro-Chemicals, Agricultural Non-point Source Pollution, Rural Revitalization and Innovation, Research Integrity and Academic Norms, Thesis and Scientific Paper Writing, Advances in Resource Utilization and Plant Protection and Organic Farming. In early 2020 I finished most of the courses. All courses mentioned above included some practical activities or study visits and I successfully passed all the courses listed above.

Preparation of the defense proposal

At the end of May, I met with my supervisor to discuss my research topic.

My supervisor Professor Yongliang Chen, gave several suggestions, and in the end we both agreed to focus on the effect of nitrogen management on maize yield and nitrogen use efficiency. I started to develop my project, since the time was very short. After interaction with supervisor, he advised and encouraged me that I would be working with a Chinese partner PhD student, that we would both be involved in conducting experiments in Quzhou and collecting data through surveys of small local producers.

Departure to Quzhou

On June 2, 2020, we set out from Beijing to Hebei province specifically to the Quzhou Experimental Station to develop research related to the process of technology transfer to small rural producers, how they design the technologies transferred by CAU students and scientists, thus contributing to their increased production and productivity. The training was held for six months at the Quzhou Experimental Station.

The trip went very well and we arrived at the destination around 4:00 pm. We were welcomed with great joy by various entities, including representatives of the center and other workers. Then, the record of our arrivals was made at the local authorities. And then we were indicated where the dormitories, cafeterias, kitchens, etc, were.

In the same period, we had a meeting with the coordinator of the project who helped us to understand the regulations and the functioning of the center. During the meeting, we also learnt, about the design of the work that will be developed throughout our stay at the Quzhou Experimental Station, how to contact with local producers and how to establish STB in Africa based on China's experience which is giving success. He also stressed the flexibility of the work and the efforts being made to integrate various supervisors who could support students in Africa.

Orientation and field visit

The next day at 8:30 am, an orientation was given by Professor Xiaoqiang Jiao to make us understand the existing infrastructure in the Quzhou Experimental Station. Following the orientation was a tour around the station: the wheat field that was in the harvest phase, parking lots of machines, field, sewage water treatment center for the reuse in the fields of crops, greenhouses among other strategic locations of operation of the station.

Improving the research proposal: Corn production and efficiency in the use of nitrogen

The time was increasingly scarce and tight, so it was very essential to accelerate the process of researching and reading various articles to connect my dissertation proposal. However, it was telling and improving that one of the most outstanding elements in this research was to have more knowledge of corn production in the world and its usefulness in the efficient use of nitrogen. It concludes that corn is a cereal of great economic and strategic importance among the cultivated grains, especially because its widerspread use is related to the agro-industrial production chain of poultry and pigs, as a product of animal feed.

Among the cereals cultivated in the world, corn is the most expressive in terms of productivity, due to its physiological characteristics and also because it is possible to obtain more than one cereal crop per year. Hence it is extremely important to understand that the different systems of maize production must be improved to achieve an increase in productivity and profitability of farmers. One of the factors that can contribute to this increase and improvement of the efficiency in the production of corn is the nitrogen fertilizer, among which urea is the most used and the most subject to nitrogen losses. This nutrient is quantitatively the most demanded by the corn crop, having a high cost in its production and very variable efficiency due to numerous factors.

The application of variable rate inputs in precision agriculture considers the spatial variability of soil fertility, through factors such as nutrient content, plant population, among others. This form of application provides inputs according to the specific needs of each portion of the crop, and the great differential is the application in variable rate does not work with averages, as in conventional agriculture, but rather generating specific data.

Through the application of nitrogen at a variable rate, it is possible to obtain an optimized fertilizer utilization, allowing the best efficiency in the utilization of this nutrient by the plant.

This type of application gives the producer several benefits, among which are the increases of profitability, optimization of the product, less damage to the environment and application during cultivation. This information in the general sense significantly helped in the improvement and conduct of the test in a very effective and efficient way.

Seeding in the corn test field Quzhou

The activities in the maize test began on 11 June and the sowing process ended on 12 June, being carried out by the workers assigned to the 300mu experiment centre. I was invited to participate in the process of sowing corn in the last phase. In this test field there were several tests, and my test was located in the same field, only what differed from each other were the treatments. The entire process of field preparation and sowing activities were carried out by the workers.

The sowing was done by means of the machines. The population density of plants in each block was 5,000 plants. In this field I concentrated on two treatments: conventional corn and optimized corn. The difference between the two treatments was the amounts of nitrogen dose that one applies more quantity and the other less quantity. The conventional practices of local farmers are to apply high doses of nitrogen at 250kg/ha and the straws are totally removed, in how much the optimized keep—whether there is a reduction in the use of nitrogen to 185kg/ha or whether there is a certain optimisation in the growth stages of plants to meet the required needs of this element in an optimal time.

Thus, it was necessary to perform this study to compare the dose of N that best contributes to the increase of maize production using nitrogen efficiently. One of the parameters was evaluated in the study: Leaf areas, stems, high plants, biomass, N-leaf content, N uptake, yield and NUE. I started collecting data on V6, VT, R1, R5 and R6 (harvest index).

Visit to STB-Xianggong Zhuang Primary School

On June 4 at 8:00 am after breakfast, we gathered in front of the dormitories, ready to visit the apple and grape growers, the purpose of which was to observe the activities being carried out by the local producers in conjunction with the Quzhou Experimental Station and other entities supporting the existence of this institution and other actors ensuring its operation. Then we left when it was 8:15 am, a total of nine students with the destination for the apple growers, having reached the destination around 9:00 am. Upon arrival, we were greeted with great courtesy and joy followed by a presentation and visit to Xianggong Zhuang Primary School.

At the beginning of the orchard, it is essential to plant healthy seedlings grafted with clonal rootstocks or seeds of the apple tree itself. As a perennial crop requiring cross-pollination, interplanting varieties should be combined in planting. I noticed that in this field school there were three types of apple varieties, each of which has extremely different characteristics and have undergone some genetic transformations that make them more delicious.

In this school we were received by the school representatives who explained how it works and the activities within the school. In this STB, I could observe a production of a grape and peach of high quality and there were different varieties with their respective flavours.

Introduction to the course Plant Protection

Professor Hongyan Zhang started the course of Resource Utilization and Plant Protection technology. He explained the essence of the course and its objective. He also pointed out that the course will have a 45-day duration and other teachers will be invited to discuss some topics.

Agricultural resources

Agriculture resource is divided into two parts:

• Natural resource—This component aims to evaluate the rational use of resources and the use of the earth sustainably so that future generations can take advantage of it, because in China the land is very limited and scarce factor. The natural factors referred to include: light, heat, water, soil, fertilizer and air.

• Economic and social resources—For a sustainable and market-oriented agriculture it is necessary to take into account some factors: capital, labour and technology. These factors will contribute significantly to increased production and productivity, if there is a multifunctional team working for development and ensuring food security.

The visit to Quzhou water resource management

The program of the day was to visit Quzhou the water resource management, the purpose of which was to observe how water is being conducted from the primary source to various points where farmers are located (river irrigation, network of rivers, well irrigation, sprinkling irrigation and mulching, water culture system in greenhouse and drip irrigation, and so on). We were involved in various activities of the course that had always culminated with some study visits and visits to other areas in order to complement and sensitize the theory of the practice.

Proposal defense of Sino-African STB master's student

On June 25th, we met in the Quzhou International Building's meeting room to defend our proposals.

My proposal was the effect of nitrogen management on maize yield and NUE, a very interesting and popular theme. I presented the proposal very well and had interaction with the members of the committee, who in turn gave some comments and suggestions on my presentation which were essential for improving my proposal.

Field test management

During my stay in Quzhou, I was involved in the process of conducting my experiment in the designated center 300mu, where the data collection process was done at the beginning of July when the plants had 6 leaves (V6) and then in VT, R1 and R6 (harvest). The application of fertilizers, spraying, tools and other cultural activities was done by the workers of the centre allocated to the experiments.

Previous results obtained so far indicated that the optimal treatment obtained the greatest result, i.e., the data show significant difference in the LAI parameter, plant height, fresh biomass, dry biomass and yield as compared to conventional treatment in all the steps. Only stem in both treatments showed no significant difference.

After finishing rehearsal in October, I was involved in other field activity, helping my colleagues whose experiment was still going on. The support I gave to the trials in my colleagues' fields was precisely to learn about the various techniques applied and to master them in both the field and laboratory activities. However, in the same period I conducted a survey in the Wangzhuang STB with the objective of investigate the quantity of fertilizers applied by small producers in the increase of production and productivity and the constraints found in the whole productive cycle.

During my stay in the Quzhou Experimental Station I made visits to various locations, STBs, companies, etc. I can affirm that I can use techniques I have learned and transfer them very efficiently in my country to contribute to the increase of production and productivity in general and especially help small producers to jump from the low-income scales.

Preparation of return to Beijing

On the 23rd of November around 8:00 am, we left the Quzhou Experimental Station and went back to Beijing. Before departure' there were several photo sessions together with most of the workers of the experimental station in several strategic locations: the international building of Quzhou, the greenhouse, the laboratory near the center museum. Finally, at the entrance gate of the station. Thus, the final point of the photo session was marked and we got into the car and left Quzhou.

Every student has a unique story, and each story consists of many sometimes small, sometimes great, but all different and interesting experiences. We enjoy learning from other people, and here is my story—hope you'll enjoy it too.

My journey to achieving my goals: Study in China

Erick Emmanuel Kumari

In 2016, when I was in my final year, I saw one big challenge with employment opportunities. All jobs require working experience for one to secure a job opportunity. I felt very stressed that one being a fresh graduate is required to have working experience. In that year I applied in 2016 to attend an agriculture business training in Israel 2016 and 2017. I secured that opportunity and I got to experience modern irrigation technology and growing vegetables in the greenhouse—soil preparation, planting, weeding, pest monitoring, spraying, operation of the irrigation system, pruning, harvesting, sorting, packing and shipping which changed my agriculture/farming life. I understood the power of youth regardless of gender in fostering the development of any country especially African countries through youth engagement in productive activities, leadership, youth-led initiatives to involve young men and women to take part in actions for change to themselves and the community.

In 2018, I decided to attend another agriculture training in the United States of America to learn about greenhouse agronomy and automation, irrigation scheduling, growing vegetables and microgreen (underrated and underutilized horticultural crops) in the greenhouse and cold frames I served in a grower position. During my time in Israel and USA I got an opportunity to work together and learn from each other with youth from 15 different nationalities around the world.

In 2019, after finishing my training, my friend and I came up with an idea of helping other youth to improve their career through gaining in real-hand experience with different farms across the country even crossing international borders by developing a program called the National Internship Program.

39

This was the deliberate efforts of transforming Tanzania agriculture in which 75% of the population involve direct. Thereafter, we helped the Tanzania government to achieve SDGs goals and in a sustainable way like China.

The reasons for applying to be a Master's student in China

After a thorough observation of the agriculture industry in Tanzania, we came to realize there are two groups of stakeholders that need to cooperate. One group is youths (mostly agriculture graduates) who have farming knowledge, time to perform farm activities. Another group is investors/hosts who own farms and have the capital to execute farm projects but they don't have time and knowledge for proper farming. You can imagine that a rapid growing population country like Tanzania and Sub-Saharan Africa countries where agriculture is dominated by smallholder farmers, developing innovative technology and transforming scientific knowledge into action for smallholder's farmer is a crucial step in addressing this challenge and sustainably feeding itself, and the world at large.

Through working with fellow youth, in April, 2019, we came to meet with this idea of Science and Technology Backyards (STBs) from China Agricultural University which works similarly to National Internship Program. Furthermore, STBs link more stakeholders than our initiative that triggers stronger desire to apply for master study in China.

Life itself drives us where we deserve to be. All you need is to have a plan, commit to your goals, prepare, be consistent and have faith. My story is one example. After establishing our initiative, we started looking at how we can reach and involve as many people as possible rather than focusing on youth only.

How the master program in Africa (Africa-STB) matched with my goals

And the only answer to my search was the Science and Technology Backyard (STB) master program for Africa (Africa-STB) which is initiated by China Agricultural University based on the ten-year practice in China. It has demonstrated considerable success in increasing crop production with high resource use efficiency, while also empowering smallholder farmers. To develop technology innovation and knowledge transfer in rural area with the STB model and empower smallholder farmers in Africa has Africa-STB master program: (1) To develop a novel model of conducting technology innovation in Africa's rural areas and make knowledge localized to Africa; (2) To develop a new model of knowledge transfer for empowering smallholder farmers and to enhance agricultural transforming towards sustainable intensification in Africa; (3) To foster high-level young people working in agriculture for sustainable development.

The arrival to China

Arriving in Beijing hasn't been an easy step in my life, not even a small one. Since the moment I stepped on this land, I was exposed to a new language which I didn't understand. It was impossible for me to ask directions, order food, communicate with people, so I didn't feel at home. My first week in Beijing was hard because the customs are not the same as in my country. When I needed help, the local people tried to help me, but there was a lack of communication. It was a miracle how I survived the first weeks with my fellow African students. As a result of those days, I was determined to learn Chinese no matter what, because I don't want to remain a foreigner for the rest of my experience in China. It's important to know the language, so I needed to sacrifice a lot in the first semester of my master's in China Agricultural University, which means attending classes from Monday to Sunday—a heavy workload for me, and I didn't have time to relax.

My decision to study in China

My decision to study in China was based on the great STBs achievements, academic facilities, global standards of education and research, and long historical friendly relationship between our two countries (Tanzania-China). In addition of my search, I looked for the best agricultural universities with high rankings and renowned faculties, learning the procedure to apply to China Scholarship Council. After reading about the faculty and the school's research achievements, I shortlisted China Agricultural University.

Also, work plan of the training. In the first year, the students should stay in China for theory learning, courses and practical skill from STB. The students will master the basic skills of agronomy and propose how to build a STB in Africa. In the second year, students proposed to go back home countries to build a new STB with the help of supervisors, local government, company and NGOs, make investigation, do field trials and provide service to local farmer based on program and local conditions. And they will get some data from farmer surveys and field trials in farmers' field for the thesis. In the third year, the students proposed to return to China to finish the thesis and graduate from China Agricultural University, then went, back home country (Tanzania) and help to push the agriculture transformation.

What is the Science and Technology Backyard (STB) in China?

Science and Technology Backyard (STB) in China is a hub that connects the scientific community with the farming community to facilitate information exchange and innovation. Science-based management technologies are brought by STB staff and discussed with leading farmers, and the latter provide feedback which is then addressed, resulting in farm-applicable recommendations. Through the hub, government and agri-businesses also engage and improve their services. STB model is an effective approach to solve the "last kilometer" problem by mobilizing resources from government, enterprises and universities. Chinese educational institutions have made their mark globally, attracting students and professionals from around the globe. A typical STB in a rural area has the following elements: First, a backyard located near farmers, houses or in a village common area. This backyard should be located in a place easily accessed by local farmers to ensure easy access of communication with agronomy experts, and it should provide some infrastructure for office work, testing, and living. Secondly, at least one expert, such as a professor, graduate student, or extension worker lives in the backyard and is available to communicate with local farmers at any time. Thirdly, advertising equipment, such as a village intra-broadcast system, cell phones, waterproof posters, and other technologies, used to disseminate science-based technology to the farm community. Fourthly, field trials test recommended technologies for sustainable intensification, and farmers manage the trials while researchers monitor farmers' practices. Fifthly, demonstration fields serve as live exhibits for local farmers, and key practices for sustainable intensification are outlined by extension workers on field days, which are held each month during the growing season. STB employs a new approach for bottom-up innovation and development of novel technologies related to sustainable intensification.

My experience at China Agricultural University as a student

The campus life in Chinese universities is rich, colorful and fulfilling. You will find campus life in China vibrant and welcoming with many opportunities to get involved in events and activities that might attract and interest you. Nearly all the universities have provided various fully equipped facilities for the convenience of students for spare time sports activities. When international students decide to study in China, they are embarking on a new journey of study life and step out of their comfort zone. They will be trained to be more independent and flexible, enjoy the unexpected and meet new people and cultures from many countries around them.

Practical field education in Quzhou Experimental Station

We understand that tertiary education is not just about time spent in lecture rooms. It's more than that. It's emphasizing the social spaces available to you, and the activities, societies and students' associations that you join. It's about gaining well-rounded experience with new friends from across the world. It's also about feeling safe and comfortable in your surroundings and conducive study environment that count. In my case, I spent my first semester in class and the second semester doing field experiment at Quzhou Experimental Station for six months.

I arrived in Quzhou county, Handan, Hebei, six months ago, with a mixed set of emotions and a thirst for new experiences and knowledge. Being given the opportunity to learn by doing at Quzhou Experimental Station had made me ecstatic beyond belief, as I have always wanted to visit a China village for its rich culture and long history. However, in the midst of the trip from the China Agricultural University, Beijing to one of its experimental station in Quzhou county, the reality that I had arrived in a new village with rural local people hit me. Coming from Tanzania, a country with a population of 58 million people, it was hard to comprehend. By the time I was in my dorm room at the experimental station, I was anxious, perplexed and fearful about how I could adjust without being able to speak Mandarin. Would I be able to explore Chinese culture and everyday life while studying? How was I going to figure out the farmers' language? What would I eat, if I couldn't ask what's on the menu or read the words myself? A hundred more questions kept me up the whole night.

Armed with a helpful orientation guideline provided by Prof. Xiaoqiang Jiao, I embarked on a trip to explore the experimental station and study the layout. The experimental station was huge with beautiful gardens, a field experiment and greenhouse, walkways, student facilities, canteens and a small shop outside; this was the China Agricultural University experimental station I had dreamed of attending.

Within a month of my arrival in Hebei, I was lucky enough to visit STB station, long-term experiment in Quzhou county. For better understanding, let us look at the origin history of the Quzhou Experimental Station and how STBs were established.

The origin history of the Quzhou Experimental Station and how STBs were established

It was in 1973 that a group of young teachers at China Agricultural University responded to the call of the Party Central Committee and the State Council to serve the country with science and technology and stay away from the capital, Beijing and friends, and came to Quzhou County, Hebei Province, and began experimental demonstration of sustainable development of agricultural production and new technologies from agricultural soil improvement rule base to practice. Quzhou County came after the experimental station. Over the past 40 years, the China Agricultural University and the people of Quzhou have fought side by side and made great achievements. "First there was the experimental station, and then there was Quzhou County." Wang Huaiyi, a villager in Wangzhuang, agreed with this sentence very much. In the past, he was so poor that he barely had enough to eat. What county is Quzhou? After the alkali was cured, Quzhou built a ton-grain county, which was called Quzhou County. In autumn, a group of young teachers from Beijing Agricultural University (the predecessor of China Agricultural University) including Shi Yuanchun, Xin Dehui, Tao Yishou, Lei Huanqun, Lin Pei, Huang Ren'an and other young teachers came to the "Laojian Nest" in Quzhou County-Zhangzhuang Jianzhan carry out research on comprehensive treatment of drought, waterlogging, alkaline and salinity. Under the difficult conditions, the China Agricultural University conducted in-depth field investigations, accumulated a wealth of first-hand information, summed up the experience and lessons of alkali control at home and abroad, and proposed that "the semi-arid and semi-humid monsoon region had an independent natural management and ecological system" theory, eventually developed a master plan that focused on combining forestry and water management through the implementation of shallow grooves and ditches.

My learning experience with Chinese farmers through STB

The Science and Technology Backyard is a comprehensive platform in rural areas that integrates agricultural technology research, farmer services, and postgraduate comprehensive skills training which was established by the local and China Agricultural University. In the past five years, they have successively established 40 science and technology institutes in 18 provinces and cities across the country, forming a national network of Science and Technology Backyards. There are many graduate students in the STBs. They first went to the STBs to familiarize themselves with the local conditions and farmers' needs. After the school started, they studied for half a year in the school, and then went to the countryside to help farmers solve various problems that they may face when farming. STB (a research platform with farmer in China) is a new platform for agricultural science & technology innovation, social service and talent training. In 2009, Professor Li Xiaolin of the School of Resources and Environment of China Agricultural University and others established the first Science and Technology Backyard in Quzhou County in order to promote high-yield and high efficiency Double high, DH technology to play a greater role in agriculture in Quzhou county. China Agricultural University centers on resources, environment and food security while Quzhou County builds a high yield and high efficiency technology demonstration base for wheat and maize. The Quzhou model, which takes high yield and high efficiency as the core, the science and technology institute of experimental station as the carrier, and the cooperation between county and school as the platform, is gradually expanding to the whole country. STB works with student and scientists from university and institute and staff from local extension department who live in STB. Investigations about the factors that limit crop yield and resource use efficiency, carry out experiments in farmer's field, modify the technologies, build up demonstration zone and show the effect of the DH technologies, introduce new machines and products (fertilizer) to simplify the DH technologies, train the farmers through different ways (face to face, organization of the farmers, giving the farmers management suggestions) to help themuse the DH techniques), and realize both high yield and high resource use efficiency and then back for investigation. As an African STB student, I am looking forward to introducing STB in my country and work hand in hand with farmers to solve existing problems and improve yield.

Wangzhuang STB

Quzhou Wangzhuang STB's main tasks are as follows: Firstly, wheat-maize high-yield and high-efficiency technology integration and demonstration and promotion model innovation. Secondly, opening farmer field schools, systematically training farmers, organizing cultural activities to improve farmers' spiritual and cultural life quality. Thirdly, developing research and demonstration of the whole process of mechanization of agricultural production. Fourthly, to explore the cooperative organization model and promote the large-scale production of food crops. STBs cooperate with each other to form high-yield and high-efficiency wheat and corn demonstrations, and achieve large-scale land use. Wangzhuang agricultural production is fully mechanized, improving agricultural production efficiency, reducing production costs, and saving labor. It improves agricultural straw utilization efficiency, and promotes the development of the local biomass fuel processing industry. These are some of the achievements achieved in Wangzhuang Village STB. It has achieved 15 innovative and integrated technologies, introduced 13 agricultural machines, and basically realized the mechanization of the whole process of food production. It developed winter wheat water and nitrogen backward technology, spring grass autumn control technology, soil testing formula fertilization, wide-range seeding technology, and summer corn watering. The research on planting technology and double-season corn planting model has formed high-yield and high-efficiency technical regulations for different planting models; the technology has radiated 5 surrounding villages, covering an area of more than 20,000 mu. It assists wheat cooperative to develop into a provincial demonstration cooperative; sets up farmer field schools to regularly train and improve farmers' scientific quality; carries out farmers' high-yield competitions, and the output of summer corn is as high as 948kg/mu, which is a record high in the past years; encourages graduate students to contract land and conduct technical integration demonstrations to gain the recognition of local farmers and the attention of the media.

My field trip at Qianya STB (grape village)

Qianya STB is one of China Agricultural University (CAU) focus villages for knowledge transfer from scientists to farmers. Historically, the village has a record of growing grapes. However, the problems of continuous grape monoculture, flood irrigation, use of poor-quality manure have led to a decrease in productivity. Generally, the farmers grow a variety known as Jufeng, which is high yielding but has been fetching low prices from the market due to poor quality. Due to these problems and the losses incurred in producing this variety, the farmer leader from this village Mr. Long approached CAU for scientific assistance.

What and how Qianya STB has done so far: Firstly, soil analysis was the key measure, to investigate the available soil nutrients and recommend new fertilizer rate applications to reduce nutrients toxicity which reduces crop yields. Secondly, introduced fertigation technique as a substitute for flooding irrigation which saves irrigation water by 70%, and fertilizer as follows: N-50%, P-39.7%, and K-40.6%. Thirdly, they introduced crop covering technique by plastic film and bagging. Plastic film controls weeds hence no herbicide required, and it maintains soil temperature and soil moisture necessary for plant growth. Fruit bagging protects fruits from burning and damage caused by extreme sunlight and insect-pest. Fourthly, the introduction of six new grape varieties: high-quality, high yielding, and disease resistant. Fifthly, improved soil health; they introduce intercropping techniques by intercropping grapes and onions or strawberries and use decomposed manure which has less risk of containing harmful micro-organisms compared to undecomposed manure. Sixthly, demonstrations, training, and farmer field schools are the key methods of transferring knowledge from researchers to farmers. They organize training now and then through PPTs and videos to ensure they transfer every knowledge of the need to the farmers because seeing is believing! Also, they highlighted a few achievements reached so far, to mention a few: the grape yield has increased from 2t/mu to 5t/mu; the introduction of a new variety of high quality which has a high price in the market increases farmers' income and reduces production cost; fertigation and plastic film have saved labor cost by 300 yuan/mu and 400 yuan/mu respectively where a farmer can save 700 (yuan/mu·year) if they adopt the newly introduced technology, summing up to 10,000,000 yuan if the whole village does adopt the new improved technology; they successfully improved soil quality and solved nutrients toxicity problems.

Lastly, one of our colleagues summarizes in her own words the lesson gained upon visitation, that "living with farmers understanding how STB works is worth an investment!" It gives the chance to understand the root problems faced by farmers and their possible solutions; it also gives you a chance to understand farmers' common behavior, a key aspect to consider enhancing the transfer of knowledge.

Linking to the agricultural problem in Africa, STB is a new way of innovation in helping local farmers from local farming methods to modern farming systems by using machinery, improved variety, nutrient use efficiency, and cropping system.

My field trip at Dezhong STB

Dezhong STB is another China Agricultural University (CAU) focal village for knowledge transfer from scientists to farmers. Historically, the village has a record of growing grapes. However, the problems of continuous grape monoculture, flood irrigation, lack of nutrients, more types of fertilizer, excessive growth, low fruit set rate, use of poor-quality manure have led to a decrease in productivity. Due to these problems and the losses incurred in producing this variety, the farmer leader from this village approached CAU for scientific assistance. Dezhong STB was established in April 2018 at Dezhong grapeyard in Quzhou town, Quzhou county, Handan city. The construction mode for this STB is the University-Agricultural-Enterprise.

The general objectives for the establishment of this STB are: to take the Dezhong grapeyard with the goal of green production and industrial prosperity and the STB as the driving force for the development, study the quality improvement and green development integrated technology model under the large grape planting system, to use the internet of things technology standard to solve the problem associated with large-scale planting, promote the whole process of the grape production and explore the green development and modern production of agriculture, thereby boosting the green industrialization of greenhouse grapes.

China has made an impression on my heart

All that has happened to me after arriving in China has made an impression on my heart. The Chinese people are full of hospitality, genuinely cooperative, wise, with a welcoming nature. All concerns I had in my mind about the language barrier or other difficulties were proved wrong. Science and technology are at the center of day-to-day life in China. You can see it in schools, streets and homes. The fact that a nation of over one billion people can live without hunger has been key to the good health and hard work of the people. Science and Technology Backyards should not be Hi-Tech for it to be appropriate. My country Tanzania needs to use science and technology backyard to use its basic raw material not to compete but to be competitive in building an agriculture industry that is suitable for its people with their levels of education.

The most precious life lesson I gained

The most precious life lesson I gained since moving to China is to develop a positive attitude and not to limit yourself based on attitude, finances and dreams. Dream big, get creative with a small budget and have a positive attitude, and it will make studying abroad memorable. My time in China has made me realize my passion for learning about other cultures, taught me not just the importance of learning in the classroom, but also of learning from every single person you meet. I look forward to the remaining time in China, and hope to visit the Great Wall, Forbidden City, among other sites, and create beautiful memories and friendships that I will cherish for the rest of my life.

From Africa to Asia: My China's life experience

Christina Lemson Hambo

It all started with an email of confirmation that I was admitted to China Agricultural University (CAU) in Beijing, the capital city of China. It was 2019 when I was admitted to join the class of African students under Science and Technology Backyard (STB) program-2019 to pursue MSc. Resources, Environmental Science and Plant Protection.

Based on remarkable agricultural development in China, for a long time I have been interested in studying in China. China counts for 20% of the world's population, and it has been able to attain food sufficiency with very limited resources of 9% of world arable land and only 6.5% of world water resources. Additionally, the country produces 25% of the world's agro-product and it has been able to feed 20% of the world's population. Such achievements has always aroused my interest in studying in China.

So, in September 2019, I received the scholarship funded by China Scholarship Council (CSC) to join China Agricultural University (CAU) to pursue MSc. Resources, Environmental Sciences and Plant Protection. This was what I wanted, but I was more curious about my new life in China since I was not familiar with Chinese culture, Chinese food and other related things.

Studying and career development

China is the global leading country in science and technology while China Agricultural University is the second largest agricultural university worldwide. Staying in China and pursuing my studies at such a university was the best option and most wonderful experience in my life. The relationship between teachers and students is wonderful and well organized. All the teachers and professors are so cooperative and helpful to students. All students are encouraged to learn and participate in different school activities like cultural and academic exchanges, workshops and different international conferences for their career development.

Lectures from professors and other experts were very interesting, informative and helpful for knowledge gain and experience sharing. My participation in different international conferences and workshops organized by CAU and other organizations has expanded my research network with other experts and researchers all over the world.

For my career development, I have always been active in participating in different international conferences organized by CAU and other organizations. On 18th October, 2019 I was invited as the guest speaker at The Road and Cooperation of Science and Technology Organization Conference in China with the topic "Ecological Restoration in Africa"; on 12th December, 2019 I attended Youth Leadership Dialogue: China – Africa Agricultural Cooperation Conference; on 25th April, 2019 I attended International Webinar: Earth Day: "The way forward on Climate and Health (COVID 19) – an online meeting; and on 30th-31st May 2021, I attended The 6th Global Youth Leadership Program 2020: Nurturing Leaders, Transforming Lives, a two-day online meeting. Furthermore, I have also been the best student on daily work reports. Participation in different international conferences has exposed me to different leaders and scientists around the world which has expanded my thinking and improved my ability and I gained new experience in different agricultural research areas, leadership and environment.

Quzhou Experimental Station experiences

In addition to the courses we undertook for the whole semester in Beijing, we had a chance to going to Quzhou Experimental Station in Hebei province, for practical sessions. From the field trials we conducted there, I am now equipped with enough knowledge and practical experience, research skills and ability to conduct field experiment successfully. In addition to the practical experiences we gained from different practical experiments conducted there, we also had an opportunity to visit different STB villages on different field trips and excursions.

STB village visitation

We visited different STBs like Wangzhuang STB, Qianya STB and Dezhong STB. At Wangzhuang STB we learnt and participated in mechanical wheat harvesting using a combine harvester machine. Combine harvester machines had the ability to perform all activities like cutting, threshing, winnowing and giving out clean wheat grains at the end. Qianya and Dezhong STB villages are commonly known for grapes production. The visitation was mainly for learning techniques and technology important for higher grape production and management practices necessary for increasing grape production. One of the major challenges in such STBs which hindered grape productivity was poor soil nutrients caused by excessive fertilizer application, poor irrigation practices like flooding and low EC causing poor soil health hence poor soil biodiversity. In Dezhong STB more advanced technologies were used such as remote sensing for measuring soil moisture, humidity, temperature, CO_2 concentration and sunlight intensity. Other technologies introduced by STBs to solve problems include optimum fertilizer application and EC-based fertilizer application which in turn increases grape yield hence improving farmers' income.

Excursions and field trips

As part of learning out of the class, we had different class trips where I had an opportunity to explore more on different agricultural-related issues. As part of the course Resource Use and Utilization, we visited different water resources management centers in Quzhou county to see how they manage water resources. Since water is a very scarce resource in China and for consideration of other factors like socio-economic factors, drip irrigation is the most recommended irrigation mode rather than traditional flooding irrigation mode since it saves water, reduces production cost but also it reduces the incidence of fungal diseases in the crops.

Another trip was to visit the Lixiang mushroom production company visitation for commercial mushrooms production. Before the trip, we had a lecture session at Quzhou Experimental Station by Prof. Suyue Zhang, where she quickly introduced how commercial mushroom are being produced using agricultural waste products. Actually, the process of mushroom production involves different procedures like substrate preparation, fermentation, sterilization, inoculation, bagging, spawning and other management. The most common substrate used includes maize brans, wheat straw, rice straw and others. Soon after the lecture, we headed to Lixiang mushroom company and learnt more on the technologies used for mushroom production. Moreover, we had a chance to see some of the mushrooms at the early harvesting stage.

Cultural exchanges

There were 34 students in our class in total from 8 African countries with different native languages, however, that was not all. I also met different people from different continents all over the world. After arriving in China, I was wondering why most Chinese couldn't speak English and that was the major challenge to me. I was asking myself "How could I live in a place where I couldn't communicate with the residents?"I asked again "How can I make friends?" My Chinese friend told me that Chinese people are very charming and welcoming people, they will always be happy to start a conversation and they love to help foreigners when asked for directions, type of foods and sometimes joking around, however language might be a huge barrier, so she said you should better learn simple Mandarin. I always wanted to make new friends so I tried very hard to learn Mandarin and fortunately, it worked out! Something funny which I was always enjoying to do is eating with using chopsticks—it was not easy at first, but then I made it. I was so happy to undertake the course Elementary Chinese and China Panorama. I still remember the funny moments of practicing Chinese in front of the class (dialogues) and writing Chinese characters—it was not easy but I finally made it. Later on, I managed to make a lot of Chinese friends, I was always enjoyed to attend Chinese festivals like "Chinese New Year" and other festivals. Attending Chinese festivals, learning Chinese language, and making Chinese friends has been helping me a lot on learning new things and adapting to Chinese culture easily.

Unforgettable moments of my stay in China

Actually, every second of my stay in China is memorable. However, I will mention three most unforgettable moments of my stay in China: COVID-19 outbreak period, proposal defense day and snowfall.

COVID-19 outbreak period

It was February when we were required to stay indoors as a means to prevent the spread of disease. It was forbidden for all international students to go out of the school without any official permission. All foods and other necessities were purchased online. Those who felt so lonely were advised to go to the playing ground inside the school gate for workout and other sport games. At this time, I used to talk to my supervisor Prof. Junling Zhang and I remember she advised me to use such a precious time to do something meaningful for my career. It's during that time that I did a meta-analysis on fertilization under different cropping systems: "Effects of bio-fertilizer on cereal-legume intercropping over sole cropping". After finishing my meta-analysis study, I then told myself, it was worth staying indoors.

Proposal defense Day

25th and 26th of June 2020 were the days set for Sino-African STB Masters Students Proposal Defense. I presented on the first day. My research proposal topic was "Investigating the impacts of phosphorus application on grain yields, and soil-P distribution under different cropping systems in China". I still remember how nervous I was, but then I remember the way I calmed myself "Tina, don't worry, you can do it." So, with time, I got myself relaxed and after I got to the stage for presentation I was all confident and I was able to present my project within 10 minutes as the given time. My presentation turned out to be very interesting. The comments from the panelists were so helpful and positive. My presentation was one of the most concise, clear and scientifically sound proposals.

Snowfall

I have never experienced minus degrees temperatures before I came to China, maybe this is the reason why I experienced snowfall for the first time in China. This is a very rare experience in most of African countries. We have snow in Tanzania at the top of Mt. Kilimanjaro but I have never been there. So, this was my very first experience of seeing tiny ice falling from heaven, I shouted, "see, it's snowing!" I took pictures and send them to my family members and friends back in my country. Snowing, such a precious and funny experience.

About China

China is the global leading country in science and technology. Over the past few decades, China has become the second largest economy country in the world. Through this, the country has been able to transform the lives of millions of people by a fast growing economy.

Additionally, China is known for its marvelous achievements in the agriculture sector by being able to feed 20% of the world's population with only 9% of the world's arable land and 6.5% of the world's water resources. Such achievements say something about sustainable utilization of resources toward sustainable agriculture. Based on the current situation regarding the global environmental challenges, sustainable agriculture remains the only option for different countries worldwide. Different countries can learn from China's experience.

Conclusion

My stay in China has exposed me to living conditions different from my country, where I have been able to gain new knowledge and experience on how to utilize agricultural resources sustainably for a sustainable agriculture development which is the global concern now. I also learnt different agricultural techniques necessary for higher crop yields which are important for reducing food insecurity problems in African countries.

My experience in Quzhou County at Quzhou Experimental Station

Ngula David Muttendango

Journey to Quzhou Experimental Station

It was Tuesday at 7 am. My alarm rang. The day had arrived! I woke up early to pack a few clothes I had selected in preparation for Quzhou Experimental Station in rural China. I quickly took a shower, at the same time reminiscing about my stay at China Agricultural University, west campus. As the water dripped down my body, I looked up to the roof, and many thoughts came to my mind. Before I went deep in thought, I heard a loud bang on the shower stall. It was my friend Amosi Mbuji. He had been my roommate for the entire stay at CAU in Beijing. He shouted, "My friend! We are running late; Prof. Jiao Xiaoqiang will leave us." 15 minutes later I was out of the shower room and hurriedly prepared myself to catch up with Amos, who had already taken his baggage to the first floor of our hostel.

Everyone looked very excited, ready to go to Quzhou Experimental Station. I decided to take some photos in memory of the occasion. In a short while, the bus had driven into at the car park. In shock! The bus looked small with the amount of luggage that was destined in its locker. I wondered how the luggages would fit in the seemingly small bus. I quickly got myself to the front of the queue to avoid getting left behind or rather seated uncomfortably because it looked like some students would sit with their knees touching their chin due to a lack of seats.

Nevertheless, every student had a comfortable seat and we set off. As we drove out of Beijing and got closer and closer to rural China, I marveled at the road network system. "China is a great country," I uttered. In the process of thinking and analyzing where my country is missing in terms of development, I dozed off.

I woke up to the view of drying wheat in vast fields as I glanced through the window of a fast-moving bus. I knew we were getting closer. The wheat looked shorter than most varieties I had cultivated in Zambia. I figured the variety was still high yielding and just some breeding work was done to reduce its height in order to avoid lodging.

I looked at my wristwatch—it had been exactly 6 hours since we took off. My body felt tired, I wondered how many kilometers we still had to cover. 3 minutes later, the bus was turning into Quzhou Experimental Station main gate. I was amazed—it looked more developed than I had anticipated. Quickly I had to get my luggage to my new room and accompany a team of professors for a Farmer Field School (FFS) meeting that was scheduled for an afternoon launch. I was very excited for I had read several articles about Farmer Field School and was eager to see the setup in China as well as meet the farmers.

As we reached and interacted with the farmers, I couldn't get a single word. I thought I could understand Mandarin as I had taken a course in my previous semester. However, the farmers' Mandarin seemed so strange that I could barely understand. We went into the meeting place, I could remember vividly what I had read in articles and what I was seeing. The Farmer Field School consisted of 25-30 farmers, who were young and old, male and female.

A visit to Xianggongzhuang STB

It's Day Three in Quzhou Experimental Station. I woke up very early before sunset. Once more, I missed the memories of China Agricultural University, the west campus. The trend was that, in the early morning before taking a shower, I developed a habit of admiring the sky and the city from above view, my room was on the top floor of the International Student Building. Beijing, What a beautiful city!!! A hive of activity, something worth its weight in gold for Chinese people.

Quickly I organized myself in preparation for the day's outing. On the previous day I was informed to prepare for a visit to Xianggongzhuang STB. Yes, plenty has been established all over China. It's a scientific tool or approach that was developed 10 years ago by a team of professors at China Agricultural University to bridge the gap between researchers and the smallholder farmers in low productive regions with the aim of improving crop productivity in the country. It had produced tremendous results.

At exactly 8 am we started our journey to Xianggongzhuang STB. We drove for about 20 minutes and at exactly 8:20 am we were welcomed by a big landmark grafted Xianggongzhuang. Dropping off the car, my sight was delighted to the view of an old woman cleaning the surroundings. I was awe-struck by the broom she was using; I had only seen those in Chinese movies way back when I was a young boy, and here I was facing the old lady as she cleans the surrounding. "Outstanding ingenuity in these rural people", I thought, as I tried to relate with some clever ideas that I had adopted from the rural people back home. They share a common thing in character. My thought was interrupted by the temperature check personnel who wanted to check my temperature at the gate of the school. As we entered through the gate, the stage was already set for us. During this period of perilous times, it's always important to give a good gesture to your neighbor. This experience took me way back in thought, I remembered a similar experience at junior high school as I needed to give a speech to the guests in a similar atmosphere. I was nervous. Luckily, I remembered a strategy that I had adopted from my cousin. These were his words, "David! When attending functions that will require you to take the podium, please wear slightly bigger trousers so that as your legs shake at the pulpit, no one will notice them." I laughed.

Within a short while, everyone was seated and the proceedings began. We handed over gifts to pupils and ended with us participating in recreation activities such as table tennis and football with the kids. You could see the delight in the face of those kids. Unforgettable experience...

We later moved to the next destination where we had a quick tour of Zhangtong School. We toured the orchard where pupils engaged in practical agricultural learning and each landmark was explained mainly to do with principle and culture through which the school is established. I recall seeing the big picture of Confucius, the great Chinese philosopher.

We ended our tour with a light moment of laughter and taking pictures in memory of the occasion.

Demonstration of wheat harvest at Wangzhuang STB

We reached the demonstration site and everything was well set. The combine harvester was in the position to give the audience a demonstration but before the demonstration took place, Professor Jiang Rongfeng had to bring us up to speed with management practice that was implemented for the crop to reach physiological maturity. He started from the mode of a cropping system that had been adopted in this STB, a winter-wheat and summer-maize cropping system was practiced in this county. He explained how the machines had to be redesigned to suit the cropping system and I quote, "To produce high-quality wheat that can be used to make bread, noodles and so forth, we had to adopt the 4-row dense and 1-row blank system." He demonstrated in the field what that meant. At this moment I expressed a sigh of relief. I could see the ingenuity behind this system. I related how I found it difficult to plant maize behind a wheat crop because of plenty of straw that clogged the planter hopper, forcing seed not to drop out or exposed and not buried in the soil. But Professor Jiang Rongfeng's explanation and demonstration on this day had balanced my equation. "No doubt about it, it's an excellent practice." I nodded in agreement with my thought. The straw acts as natural mulch for maize which improves water retention. Many farmers back home in Zambia had argued that it does not return enough organic matter relative to other cover crops but I always stood my ground, as for several years I had noticed the merits of wheat straw improving water retention on degraded soil in several fields I had cultivated. This practice was good for water retention and thus made fertilizer available to the soil. The 4-row dense and 1-row blank method required planting wheat densely within 30cm with a row spacing of 10cm apart and the other 30cm space was left blank to be planted on maize after winter harvest. This was made possible with a GPS installed on tractors. This technology still maintained the required plant density for a high yield crop. However, professors had to formulate specific fertilizer suiting the model of this winter-wheat and summer-maize cropping system to attain high protein content, high nitrogen use efficiency, high yield, and of course to fetch a high price on the market.

Professor Cui Zhenling gave a presentation because he was the main scientist behind this technology. As he explained to the audience about the technology, you could see the humility and passion from the handsome researcher as he spoke calmly and deliberately. These professors had devoted their lives to helping and saving the farmers. He discussed how remote sensing technology is used to manage the crop in various ways ranging from detecting water stress, yield estimation, mapping disease, and insect-infested areas, and so on. He summarized the demonstration by stating that a collective approach is needed to get a high yield and increased nitrogen use efficiency. He emphasized good planters modified to fit the 4-row dense and 1-row blank system integrated with high yielding varieties, good cropping system, good harvesting machinery to prevent crop losses, good management system (remote sensing) to monitor crop growth, and stressed the importance of formulated fertilizers in this system.

After all the presentations, the most crucial and tense moment approached. It was time to start the combine harvester and know the yield. This moment is joyous to a farmer. As we waited to hear the yield that had been obtained, I looked at the eyes of the farmers, and I could relate to what was going through their mind. The stress of planting should be replaced by the joy of achieving the desired yield. The target yield had been surpassed! 9.4 tons per ha had been achieved.

Introductory lecture by Prof. Zhang Hongyan

"This drastic weather change is not good for the body," I mentioned as we exchanged thought with a colleague. We had experienced drastic weather changes in the past five days. Prof. Zhang Hongyan walked in at exactly 20 minutes past 8 am—we were to have a lecture at 8:30 am. The professor started with a quick introduction to the location of Quzhou Experimental Station. "Quzhou is a county located in the central part of Huanghuaihai Plain in Hebei province," he explained. He emphasized the importance of this region. "This region practices an intensive agriculture system and agriculture is the main activity with a winter-wheat and summer-maize cropping rotation system, so the land has no time to rest." I nodded my head in agreement. The window between harvesting winter-wheat and planting summer-maize was very short, which required farmers working for long hours to quickly harvest wheat and sow maize soon after.

Prof. Zhang Hongyan took us through the hunger history that had rocked China from the late 1890s to 1943. He recalled a touching memory between him and his mother—it was not accepted to leave food on the plate after eating. Food was the first necessity of the people. China experienced food scarcity in the 1890s to around 1945, continuous mono-cropping resulted in degraded soils to a point where no grass or trees could grow. People ate barks of trees. Many challenges were encountered by China during this period—for several times they needed to defend their country against colonial rule from the first opium war in the 1840s, the second opium war in the 1860s, and the war resistance against the Japanese from 1937 to 1945.

Because of a deep history of hunger in the past, many Chinese leaders paid more attention to food security as a national strategy. China now boasts 9% of arable land and contributes 20% cereal production, 28% meat production, contributing 22% to the world population. However, this has come at a cost of environmental pollution. Over the years grain production had increased with increasing fertilizer use especially Nitrogen and Phosphorus, but increasing yield was at a cost of excessive use of fertilizers and pesticides resulting in decreased nutrient use efficiency. The production of cereals in China will require technologies that can increase nitrogen use efficiency whilst using less fertilizer. Cost of production is another challenge facing many smallholder farmers in China. The cost of producing a ton of maize in the USA is only 700 RMB while Chinese farmers need a 2,000 RMB for the same quantity.

After the lecture we headed to the museum, where the professor started with an explanation of why Quzhou Experimental Station had to be established in Quzhou county. For many years the county faced soil salinity problems. Nothing could grow in this county and the people were very poor and survived on extracting salt from the soil as the main activity to sustain their livelihood. The government could not even collect tax in this region due to its extreme poverty status. In 1973, 6 scientists set off to live in the county with the farmers and try to solve the soil salinity problem that existed. They had to learn from the native people and then use their technical ability to solve the problem. Gradually yields started to increase from 79 kg per mu to 300 kg per mu. Over the years soil regained its fertility and currently intensive agriculture is practiced and it's the main activity of the native people.

A visit around Quzhou water resource management

I had attended two lectures by Professor Zhang Hongyan so far and I had enjoyed both. The first lecture was more of an introduction to the Quzhou Experimental Station. He ran us through the spirit of Quzhou that existed among the great scientist that lived here and sacrificed their life to solve smallholder farmers' problems. His first lecture reminded me of one thing, "everything great faces great challenges." I recalled as I went into deep thought. I remembered the struggle of the Jewish people, many years back Tel Aviv was a desolate area and life was almost impossible to live there but wonders were done and today it's the hub and birthplace of many great technologies the world has ever seen. The Negev desert is in the process of transformation to a semi-tropical climate. That great nation will always hold a special place in my heart. A similar story of triumph existed in Quzhou county.

On the third day of lectures, the professor decided to take us for an excursion around Quzhou water resource management. Water was now the key to many problems around this county. Many years back, the scientists had great success over soil salinity that impoverished this county, and now another challenge surfaced. This county had for many years practiced an intensive winter-wheat and summer-maize rotation system without resting the soils and the underground water was depleting rapidly because of flood irrigation system. This is a great challenge that faced modern scientists. It was evident that something had to be done. Many smallholder farmers had adopted and practiced the flooding irrigation that had low water resource efficiency. The problem had arisen! Food security was at risk once again in this county.

As we headed to the Huangkou Watergate, we had several stopovers just to appreciate the activities that were happening in the farmers' fields. It was clear that the mode of irrigation was a flooding system. A very outdated and inefficient irrigation technology. In a more organized system, the irrigation was well managed, and piping was well connected to the field of the farmers. All they needed was to connect their pipe and inform the water manager to start the pump and water would flood their fields. The timing of irrigation and the amount irrigated did not bother the farmer. The farmers' interests were to grow food at less cost and get their money. However, the disadvantaged farmers who were distant from the river had to drill deep water boreholes to a depth of about 250m with a water table at 80m thus increasing the cost of production. It was clear that the farmers needed help and STB was already on the ground carrying out demonstrations to train and change farmers' mindset towards sustainable water resource management.

As we reached Huangkou Watergate, we were welcomed by the site engineer. A big project was in progress for many years now. Five rivers had been connected with the help of the man-made river to create the largest control system for domestic water supply in China. It was an ambitious project that was being carried out by Chinese government. We ended our visit to Huangkou Watergate with a group photo and what felt like a successful mission.

On our way back to Quzhou Experimental Station, we had a quick visit to Qianya county. It's well known for grape farming. A demonstration was laid out by CAU STB students demonstrating how drip irrigation can solve the challenge of water shortages and simultaneously produce quality crops. Any fertilizer was applied together with irrigation, a process called drip fertigation. A clear and concise explanation was given by the student managing the field.

A visit to Qianya STB

4th July, 2020 saw five STB-Africa students visiting Qianya STB. The visit was scheduled for a morning and afternoon session. The students were accompanied by the Director of Quzhou Experimental Station, Prof. Jiang Rongfeng and the Deputy Director Prof. Zhang Hongyan. The morning session involved meeting the leader of Qianya STB. Mr. Long introduced a brief background on how the STB was established in response to the challenges that were faced by the farmers in that particular area. The afternoon session was braced with meeting the government official, secretary of Quzhou county.

The leader of Qianya was very excited to meet the STB-Africa students and had a tour with the students around the demonstration sites. Basically, establishment of Qianya STB was initiated by Mr. Long, the leader of smallholder farmers within Qianya county who faced a lot of challenges in grape production. Among many challenges was poor soil quality, excessive use of fertilizer by the farmers and poor irrigation strategies used by smallholder farmers such as flooding. Upon seeing the challenges faced by the farmers and getting hold of what China Agricultural University STB students are doing in other areas, he called for an STB to be established in Qianya.

The STB was established in 2017 with a team of two CAU students who had to rent apartments and land for demonstration trials, which was facilitated by Mr. Long. The demonstration trials were located on roadside to attract farmers, some sort of advertisement. The students started from scratch to diagnose the challenges of grape production in Qianya. The main challenge that was faced was low electric conductivity implying poor soil health and reducing soil biodiversity. The other bad management practice conducted by the farmers was flooding irrigation that spread toxicity to other places of the soil. The students initiated different management practices like fertigation, high yield cultivars to make the production profitable at the introduced technology cost.

A visit to Lixiang Mushroom Company

On 13th July, 2020 STB-Africa students visited Lixiang Mushroom Company. Before the trip, a lecture was scheduled to take place at 9:00 am from a very renowned expert in mushroom production. Professor Zhang Suyue from the Hebei University of Engineering quickly took us through an introduction to utilization of agricultural resources and mushroom production system.

After 25 minutes of lecture, we headed to Lixiang Mushroom Company and were welcomed by the managers at the company. The stuff took us through the basic production system of mushroom cultivation. We appreciated the structures used to produce mushroom and later we learned the substrates that are used to produce mushroom. The company uses a mixture of biochar, cow dung and maize hull as substrate. This material is bagged and sterilized to kill all germs and prepare to cultivate the mushroom. The substrate is later mixed with mushroom spores and bagged or spread on the mart and put in the growing house. The temperature and humidity should be well regulated to provide a conducive atmosphere for production.

The first harvest is called the first flush and it can reach up to fifth flush for a good harvest. After all the flushes of harvest are exhausted, the substrate is sold to the smallholder farmers as manure—a source of fertilizer.

Message from Suri Zhang

After studying and communicating with my good friend David, I found that there are many advantages I should learn from him. The main points are summarized: 1. Hardworking and self-disciplined. 2. Gentle, never irritable, and calm down slowly and deal with it bit by bit. 3. Emotional intelligence is very high. I feel very comfortable when I talk to him, and I like to talk to him very much, and I like to ask him when I'm in trouble. 4. He likes to eat small and frequent meals. He can eat several times a day, but the amount of food for each meal is not large, so that his blood sugar will not be high. Recently, I was reading "Dietology" by a Japanese writer. The reason why I am fat is that I eat too much. I like to eat sweet noodles, and these are the important reasons that cause my blood sugar to rise rapidly. Therefore, in the next period of time, I will strictly control my diet and health. Fruits should be placed before meals or not eaten. If you really want to eat sweets, you can choose sweet potatoes, apples, grapefruits, peaches and other sweet unprocessed foods. Walk for 20 minutes after a meal, or stand for 20 minutes. Do not let yourself sit or lie down anyway. Losing weight is not only for beauty, but also for health. Scientists say that long-term obesity is the fuse that leads to various diseases. If it is not controlled, it will produce various cardiovascular diseases, and even obesity can cause short life and aging process. Okay, this time it has completely aroused my desire to lose weight, so from today until the holiday, I hope I can lose weight quickly to keep myself healthy.

I found that I am actually not very self-disciplined, and the beginning of success is self-discipline. I often choose to rest on weekends or holidays. Even when I arrive at the library in time, I will be lazy and don't want to use my brain. Sometimes my learning enthusiasm is not enough. I need to study hard like David and keep my dreams in my heart. Therefore, when I am decadent, I should read more inspirational stories, so that I can adjust myself as soon as possible and get myself immersed in learning as soon as possible. I believe I will get better. I don't think I am the smartest one, but I want to be the most diligent one.

I have set a small goal for myself. I have to write a journal every day, not eat dinner every day (except for dinner out), and exercise for one hour; complete a set of English test questions every day and read an English document or two Chinese documents every day; a paper, and write it in the work log. Only eat carbohydrates for breakfast, choose to eat vegetables and meat at noon, and reduce the intake of rice, steamed bread and noodles. Turn off the phone at 11:30 pm every day, and the video session with David is 11:00 pm to 11:20 pm every day, otherwise it will affect sleep. There is no rest on weekends. If you feel tired, you can watch extracurricular books or short inspirational videos on Saturday morning. Be humble and respect others.

In short, I hope that two months can change me into a beautiful and self-disciplined young lady. I hope that David and I can become the most successful people, study hard, and have a successful career.

The first appearance on Chinese soil—a dream turned into reality

Jasper Kanomanyanga

Arriving at the Beijing Capital International Airport on the night of September 9th, 2019, I was completely clueless about where China Agricultural University (CAU) was and how to navigate through the very sophisticated world-class airport to my destination. Through asking a lot of strangers around the airport, I, fortunately, got into a taxi which precisely dropped me at the northwest gate of the CAU west campus in the Haidian district of Beijing. Overwhelmed by the completely new environment and travel exhaustion, I barely knew where exactly I wanted to go as I could only see masses of people and never-ending vehicle traffic around me. I was so naive and the new scenic views puzzled and confused me even more as I was stuck at the school gate. As a rule of thumb, I went to the gate officer to ask where the International Students Building was located and he kindly found a random student who took me to my final destination. Upon arrival, I was assigned to my room where I would live during my academic stay in China. As I always believe that first impressions last, I can say that I have witnessed the kindness of the Chinese people during this unforgettable night as they made my arrival a lot easier than I anticipated.

The Great Wall adventures

After some days in Beijing, another great moment came by when my colleagues and I visited the renowned Great Wall of China. The occasion was organized by the Beijing International Christian Fellowship (BICF) which is a Christian church for foreigners in China. Great Wall is a world famous feature well known for being the only man-made feature observable from space. For that very reason, it was a dream come true to have such a great opportunity to witness the great work of the ancient Chinese people to ever exist. We visited the Huairou Great Wall side in the Huairou district. Thereto, we stayed for 3 days and nights in a very comfortable hotel. During the day, we would do a lot of activities like mountain hiking along the walls, boating, and visiting some other wonderful sites around the district. The Great Wall of China is about 21, 000km long built with earth and stones using human labor. Magnificent walls of about 7m in height built along various altitudes of mountains were just a mind-blowing scene. It was generally an unforgettable and joyful adventure of my life.

The academic experience in CAU

On the academic side, we took various courses during the first year, and among them are plant nutrition, advanced experimental design and biostatistics, safe production of agro-produce, efficient utilization and management of agrochemical products, integrated management of plant pests, agricultural non-point source pollution, modern agricultural innovation, rural revitalization strategy, research integrity and academic norms, advances in resource utilization and plant protection technologies and elementary Chinese. It was quite satisfying and encouraging to be taught by professional professors and doctors of CAU and these courses gave me a clear insight into the amazing technological advancements that China had and continued to use to ensure the food security of almost 20% of the world population. Most excitingly, all the lectures were designed in an interactive way in which every student had to present on a certain topic and allow discussion among other students and the lecturer. To enhance quick understanding of concepts, we were also taken for various excursions around the city of Beijing which include the Beijing Water Works where recycling of water is done, the CAU long term experimental station where CAU students and tutors conduct their field and greenhouse experiments, the Olympic Park, only to mention a few. From all these excursions, I could now start having a clear insight of how the world renowned China looks like, although I remained curious to see other famous tourist places like the Forbidden City, Summer Palace, the Glass Bridge, etc.

One of the most interesting courses for me was Elementary Chinese. Before that I had never known even a single word/character of Chinese, although I always wished to. The course was conducted every Saturday on the east campus of CAU where almost all international students gathered for the class. Again, the class was interactive as every student had to participate in practicing to speak Chinese in front of the class. Pinyin and characters were taught during the whole semester and I managed to grasp a lot which helped me to easily adapt to the Chinese people. After about three months of learning Chinese, I could now speak with the Chinese people on different occasions like the restaurant and market although with some difficulties, and this allowed me to practice it further as I believe that practice makes perfect.

Snowfall: A rare phenomenon in Africa

Zimbabwe is a country dominated by a temperate climate with hot-wet summers and cold-dry winters. On the contrary, China is just the opposite, with freezing winter that goes down to −20℃. Snowfall was one of the amazing things I have long waited for since my landing in Beijing.

It was during the night I suddenly opened my WeChat that I found many people were already posting pictures of themselves enjoying snowfall the very night. This means I was almost late in realizing my dream had come true. Without wasting any split second, I rushed and peeped through the window and I could not believe what I was seeing. Tiny ice particles were falling from the sky like the famous biblical manner from the heavens. To make sure I was not dreaming, I took the stairs down to witness all this from outside. Mother Nature was in the midst of doing wonders as a thick layer of ice had already piled onto the surface before I knew it. I started taking pictures with my other African colleagues who were also still in shock of what we were observing. That alone made my night that I could not wait to see how it would look like the following morning. Many people woke up early to enjoy the snow and I could see many making some snowmen with the ice and taking all sorts of funny pictures around the campus.

Diaries of the invisible enemy, Covid-19

In late December 2019, there was an outbreak of the coronavirus in Wuhan, a city in Hubei province of China, which later became a pandemic. This was a total swing to every plan of our academics as many lectures were being conducted online. However, unlike other countries around the globe, China fought a relentless fight to control the spread of the virus. This included a countrywide lockdown, building of an emergency hospital in the epicenter of the pandemic in a 10-day period, en-masse coming out of healthy personnel from around the country to the seriously hit regions, timeous production, and provision of Personal Protective Equipment (PPE) among other inventions. Like any other Chinese citizens, our health as international students was of utmost importance marked by strict movement regulations and regular provision of sanitary materials and masks. For about 4 months we have been indoors while being allowed to move around the campus for exercising. This did not inconvenience our living in any way but rather protected us from any possible ways of getting infected. We could buy everything we wanted like foodstuffs, clothing, etc. online and efficiently without any challenge. The virus (Covid-19) later was overcome and became less around the country so we could be now allowed to go to the shops on regulated schedules. To me China proved that unity brings out the best as every citizen, primarily the health officials and the government cooperated tirelessly in getting rid of the Covid-19.

My journey from Beijing to Quzhou, Hebei province—internship experiences

According to the plan of our program, we were supposed to do an internship program in our home countries starting from July 2020 but everything was cancelled due to the pandemic. However, a contingency plan was put forward for us to conduct a practical internship here in China instead. On the 2nd of June, 2020, we moved from CAU, Beijing, to Quzhou Experimental Station in Quzhou county, Hebei province where we would carry out our academic field experiments as well as get exposure to China's agricultural side. Before we left CAU, we were provided with safety materials like face masks and alcohol sprays for use along the way and during our initial stay at the experimental station. The journey was a joyous and adventurous expedition as we moved from a cosmopolitan city to rural China. Many beautiful hills and buildings could be seen from a distance along the way and activities like outstanding and advanced farming systems could be viewed through the fast-moving bus. Highly developed world-beating road infrastructure was a marvel to watch as the bus changed lanes moving like a meandering river. When we arrived at Quzhou Experimental Station, we were warmly welcomed by the station staff and other students. We were allocated our living rooms which had utmost conducive studying and decent living facilities. Moments later, a group of six students went to represent us at the launch of a new farmer field school around Quzhou county. They were accompanied by two professors from Quzhou Experimental Station, Prof. Zhang Hongyan, and Prof. Jiang Rongfeng. A new crop (Stevia) was recently introduced in the surrounding villages and a farmer field school extension program was formed to facilitate adoption and intensive learning of the crop's production by the farmers. Upon returning, meal cards were provided to all of us which were to be used to access meals from the canteen throughout our stay at the experimental station.

Depending on one's choice, students who preferred to cook their meals were provided with a kitchen room. Our safety as students was still of paramount importance during that COVID-19 pandemic era and no student was allowed to go out of the station without permission and good reason. Good care was provided to us from Beijing to Quzhou and it was everyone's duty to abide by the safety rules of the Quzhou Experimental Station. Dinner was provided and after eating, we then conducted a meeting in the International Corporation Centre building where we received an official welcome from all the station officials. Rules and regulations were shared with us about our stay.

Quzhou Experimental Station orientation

On Wednesday the 3rd of June, 2020, it was my second day at Quzhou Experimental Station. This was the day to have a full glance at the research station and all its scenic sites. By 6:30 am, everyone was up, preparing to leave for the excursion around the station. The first place visited was the parking area and Dr. Jiao Xiaoqiang was taking a lead throughout. Thereto, we met some staff who were sorting out the experimental wheat samples by cutting off the spikes and pack them into labeled packs according to specific treatment for further analysis.

The experiment was done to compare organically to inorganically grown wheat on different parameters like nutrient content and quality, and grain yield. We then headed to the eastern side of the station where there are some long-term experiments underway. The first experiment was comparing the effect of applied nitrogen and phosphorous on the yield and other different parameters of wheat. The treatment where P was applied had many spikelets per spike and a clear distinct crop stand which also means higher grain yield by approximation. In N treatment, we also noticed that the crop had delayed maturity as compared to P treatment. However, in plots where both nutrients were applied, the crop vigor was high with an outstanding number of spikelets per spike. This could mean that both N and P nutrients are key limiting factors to wheat growth and development and yield although there was still a need for the statistical conclusion and scientific explanation.

The second long-term experiment was the investigation of the winter-wheat and summer-maize rotation system on its effect on yield and nutrient resource use efficiency in the North China Plain. No enough notable evidence was noticed on the performance of both crops. However, the obvious prediction was that the rotation system might be a success in improving the nutrient use efficiency as well as the yield of both crops. We proceeded to the workshop where there were a lot of modern farm implements like planters, combine harvesters, tractor-drawn plows, etc. Generally, they were all advanced types of machinery suitable for precise farming in modern agriculture. The other place visited was the northern side of the experimental station where there are farmers' fields and some students' experiments. A rare crop, especially in Africa, called stevia was under cultivation. Stevia is used as a sweetener in tea and has nutritional value especially for diabetic people. The crop was still at an early growth stage and some farmers were doing hand-weeding. The last visit was to the highest standard glasshouse where some students' experiments were also underway. We noticed several experiments that were investigating stevia, soil analysis, Chinese cabbage, etc. After enjoying the work around the station, I was left with no question on how China is managing to ensure food security for over 1.4 billion people. Agricultural research and development services are strong and efficiently run that every farming problem has been addressed. Quzhou Experimental Station is undoubtedly playing a pivotal role to ensure problems faced by the local farmers are dealt with.

First field visit: Xianggongzhuang village

On Thursday 4 June 2020, we had a great opportunity to visit the Xianggongzhuang village located a few miles away from Quzhou Experimental Station. We left for the village at around 8:45 am and arrived around 9:10 am. We were cheerfully welcomed at Xianggongzhuang Primary School by some teachers, CAU STB students, and other representatives from different companies to whom we were introduced. As a protective measure, everyone had to wear a mask and other safety measures were being practiced in the prevention of the Covid-19 pandemic. Two STB students were taking the lead on instructing and directing us to where we met with the primary students and some teachers at the school. It was one of the best moments that we experienced during our few-day stay in Quzhou county. We gathered together with the primary school kids who were so excited to meet us and have our company. Moments later, the school administration, various representatives from other companies, and our university professor started sharing some speeches. We, the STB students, and other staff then assisted in handing over some donations which included sports materials like balls and various Personal Protective Equipment (PPE) like sanitizers and face masks to the primary students and the school in particular. A few minutes after, we started having some 'mixing and mingling' activities and some funny moments with the juveniles. We played table tennis and football as a great opportunity of getting used to each other. We proceeded to one of the biggest primary schools in Quzhou county called Zhangtong Primary School. There after, we had a great opportunity to meet more new people who introduced some rare fruit trees and other activities done at that school. Finally, we took some group pictures before returning to Quzhou Experimental Station and we arrived around 11:00 am. At noon we had our lunch and went to the reading room where we continued working on our academic researches and other different stuff. Generally, we had a fruitful and wonderful time to have been exposed to Chinese culture and norms as we visited the two schools.

Wangzhuang STB field visit

On Saturday the 6th of June, 2020, we visited the Wangzhuang STB demonstration field in Wangzhuang village. The field was under the supervision of the Quzhou Experimental Station. We left the station at around 9:00 am and traveled about 6km to the farmer's wheat field. At the field, there were already some STB students, farmers, and teachers who were waiting for us (African STB students) to arrive. Prof. Jiang Rongfeng started by introducing us to some of the staff who informed us about the general field status and what needed to be done.

The total area of about 120mu (8ha) was planted a wheat variety Zhongmai578 in October 2019 and harvesting just started on the very day we arrived (June 6, 2020). This is a very special variety with an average yield of about 9t/ha, high quality and high protein content suitable for baking and other essential uses. It was planted following the new planting model technology which follows a winter wheat-summer maize crop rotation system. The wheat was planted in 4cm×10cm apart inter-rows which were separated by a 30cm wide unplanted space. Advanced equipment was used from land preparation to harvesting. A highly efficient combine harvester equipped with the GPS technology to measure area harvested and other field related characteristics was the one underuse. Remote-sensing technology was also used throughout the wheat-growing period for soil chemical analysis, plant population, yield estimation, etc. This harvester has very minimal harvest losses. After harvesting, the wheat straw is returned and minimum tillage is applied for the summer maize. The straw is further chopped into smaller sizes which will not interfere with maize germination. In summer, the minimum tillage is done by making a furrow in-between the 30cm space where wheat was not planted. Maize is then planted at 60cm inter-row spacing. This cropping system is done to improve nutrient and water use efficiency between the two crops.

After getting these explanations about the newly implemented planting model, the combine harvester then made a run of about 0.4mu (0.027ha) total area as a demonstration of the harvesting process. The wheat was bagged into 50kg bags, weighed and moisture content was determined using a moisture meter. The average moisture content was 14.2%. The yield was then calculated and the variety proved to be unique as it produced a yield of 9.4t/ha which was high enough in contrast to other local varieties which give 4-6t/ha yield on average. Samples were then taken for further lab analysis of properties like protein content, etc. This whole experiment kept showing me the other side of China's agricultural success in terms of their staple crop i.e. wheat.

Lecture continuation and the history of Quzhou Experimental Station

On Monday the 8th of June, 2020, we started a new course at Quzhou Experimental Station called advances in resource utilization and plant protection technologies. It was being conducted by Professor Zhang Hongyan from the CAU. The course covered the modern technologies that are being implemented by farmers and researchers, especially in China, to cope up with the environmental, social, and economic challenges in their day-to-day agricultural production.

Plant protection strategies and common problematic pests and diseases were also discussed. Unlike in Africa where the fall armyworm continues to ravage crops especially corn, China managed to control this notorious pest once and for all. The chemical control method is the major way that farmers in China use to control pests and diseases. Compared to recent years when the use of agrochemicals was very intensive, China realized the aftermaths that were being brought about by this and now is emphasizing the green agriculture approach. This is the use of very minimal agrochemicals and organic inputs in agricultural production to curb environmental degradation and encourage safe food production.

After the lecture, we then went to the Quzhou Experimental Station Museum where the history of this experimental station was extensively discussed. It was said that China experienced unprecedented food shortages beyond the 1970s due to insufficient agro-inputs and relevant technologies coupled with a high population. However, this among other reasons has prompted the establishment of the Quzhou Experimental Station intending to conduct scientific researches that would inturn help farmers to solve their production constraints by providing them with proper solutions and technologies. Since the establishment of the Quzhou Experimental Station in the Handan district, tremendous yields were recorded, the problem of saline soils was solved, disease incidence was managed, and land degradation was also reduced to a minimum, among other positive improvements. From the beginning of the past decade, many students mainly from the China Agricultural University continued to be trained there and many STBs have been established all over China. This evidenced a breakthrough in China's agricultural production of crops like wheat, rice, maize, etc. which resulted in food security in the country.

Irrigation water management in Quzhou

On Wednesday the 10th of June 2020, Professor Zhang Hongyan took us for an excursion around Quzhou county where we explored many of the water resource management and irrigation technologies being used by the smallholder farmers in their farming operations. Our first stop was just a few miles away from the experimental station, where farmers were just setting up their irrigation pumps and pipes to irrigate their various crops. There after, the water was being sourced from a huge tunnel which is linked to the major river in Quzhou county called Fuyang river. We proceeded and arrived at the major aforementioned river where Professor Zhang discussed how farmers were served by that big river through tunnels. The tunnels were constructed mainly to supply irrigation water to the smallholder farmers at an affordable electricity charge. Farmers who cannot access the water tunnels however use shallow and/or deep wells as irrigation water sources and pay affordable electricity charges slightly higher than that of those who use tunnel water. At the next stop along the Fuyang river, there were some underground pipes that some farmers use to pump water from the main river to their farms. It was noticeable that many farmers along the Fuyang river grow more horticultural crops like eggplant, cabbage, etc. as compared to those far away from the main river. Also, farmers close to the main river grow more crops all-year-round because of their proximity to the perennial river.

We also visited the Qianya village via some smallholder farmers' fields where shallow wells of about 30-40m deep were used as a water source for irrigation of spring maize. This is a bit expensive for the farmers as they have to pay more for the electricity utility. At Qianya village, one of the STB stations, there was grape production and the STB students from CAU were helping farmers on the good practices of irrigation that efficiently use water among other practices. The key irrigation technique was drip irrigation. The water was pumped from a deep well of about 100m deep, sieved and mixed with fertilizer (fertigation) before directed to the drip irrigation pipes. This method has proved to be highly efficient in water use efficiency (WUE) with above 90% WUE. The STB students demonstrated to us how generally grape production is done using drip irrigation and was discouraging farmers to use the traditional methods of irrigation like flood irrigation as it results in water wastage and low WUE. After that, we then made our way back to the experimental station.

In conclusion, water is one of the very scarce resources in Quzhou county, which renders the need to be efficiently managed to avoid unprecedented water losses. Many technologies are being implemented by the farmers which include plastic mulching, returning of crop residues, and other mentioned strategies to minimize water loss and improve WUE. There is, however, still a great task of educating farmers on these issues as there is still some resistance by smallholder farmers in adapting to water saving technologies.

The scariest moment—proposal defense

On the 26th of June 2020, we, the African-STB students defended our theses proposals. Three people presented before me and when my turn came, I was so nervous but I managed to get rid of the stage phobia. I presented my research titled "Assessing the challenges facing the public agricultural extension services in Zimbabwe". I presented very well and managed to finish within the stipulated time of 10 minutes. The comments and questions which came from the panelists were so valid and helpful, one of which was to specify my research objectives. Generally, the presentation was said to be concise and straight forward. After the presentations, Dr. Jiao invited us for some guidance and recommendations about our proposal presentations which had to be made in our research proposals. That was so helpful as it improved our understanding and carrying out of the researches.

The mushroom production farm visit

Waking up at 8:00 am, I got myself ready to leave for the Qiuxian district where commercial mushroom production is done. Before leaving, we headed to the lecture theatre and conducted a lecture about mushroom production for the course Utilization of Agricultural Resources. It was conveyed by Professor Zheng Suyue from the Hebei Engineering University. It started at around 9:00 am and was translated to us by her company. The duo took us through the general production procedures of mushrooms. In summary, the procedures involve the culture material (substrate) preparation (maize corncob, rice straw, wheat straw, manure, sawdust, rice bran, soil, etc.) by fermenting, sterilizing, inoculating, bagging, spawning, soil casing, and general management depending on the variety of the mushroom. During fermentation, the substrate is cured and fermented to improve its nutrient quality as well as getting rid of pathogenic organisms and weed seeds. Furthermore, the substrate is sterilized at around 125℃ for 3-4 days again to eliminate any harmful soil pathogens.

The mycelia are inoculated under 20-25℃ in a dark room until it germinates. After that, it is taken to the growing media in a dark culture room where the temperature is maintained at 20-25℃, humidity at around 80%-95%, and the air is regulated. After the lecture, we left for Qiuxian district where we had a physical appreciation of how mushroom is cultured. At the first farm, *Agaricus blazei* was under culture and at the early harvesting stage. Biochar, soil, wheat bran, and manure were used as substrate.

We proceeded to the second farm where we saw some advanced technologies in the preparation and sterilization of the substrate and how it is mechanically turned and bagged. What has been puzzling me before was seeing mushroom in almost every supermarket all year round without understanding where and how it is produced. From this day on, I now had full knowledge about the mushroom production in China as one of the huge production lines which earn higher than many crops.

Dezhong grape STB visit

On 24th July, 2020, all African and a few Chinese STB students visited Dezhong grape STB which is about 10-15 km away from Quzhou Experimental Station. Dezhong STB is an enterprise-university cooperative established in

2011 on a total area of more than 300mu. The STB program was initiated in 2018 to help the cooperative and local grape farmers in improving their yield through the provision of advanced technologies and other relevant technical support. Among these are the remote sensing technologies for the detection of temperature, humidity, soil moisture, sunlight intensity, leafy humidity, and CO_2 concentration which was also introduced by the CAU STB program. Other technologies which include optimum fertilizer application, EC-based fertilizer application, and green production technology (minimizing pesticide, fertilizer use, and supplementing of trace elements) were also introduced to the cooperative and local farmers. As a result, the establishment of the STB has seen local farmers and the cooperative noticing significant changes in grape yield, income and mitigation of soil degradation, and other managerial problems are now a thing of the past.

After the presentation, the Chinese STB students and other cooperative staff led us around the greenhouses where grapes are cultivated and further demonstrated how grapes are cultivated. We had a great time with the cooperative workers, and we were given some fruits and wine which was brewed from the same grapes.

Field maize data collection

Although it was on a Sunday, a day supposedly meant for resting, it turned out to be a more hectic day than ever. I woke up early at 5:00 am joining my colleagues in the field experiment in Wangzhuang STB. We met in front of our dormitories where they were all waiting for me. We left for Wangzhuang STB at around 5:30 am where we collected data from one of my colleagues' maize experiments and soil sample collection.

We arrived at the field at around 6 am and started cutting three maize plants from every plot of three treatments while the other team was measuring plant height, leaf lengths, and widths and recording results in datasheets. We finished collecting the data and took the samples to the experimental station where we separated the leaves from the main stems, cut the stems, and packed them into a distinctly labeled pack. The samples were then allowed to air dry in the greenhouse and soil samples were taken for oven drying.

Maize data collection with my colleague at the Wangzhuang STB outlet

My colleagues and I visited the Baizhai STB with the company of Prof. Hongyan. We left the experimental station at exactly 9:10 am for Baizhai village. There was a field day hosted by the Baizhai STB which was meant to showcase the production of corn for laying hens and high-quality eggs. High calorie and high yielding variety of maize (HappyFall368) is bred and cultivated in Baizhai STB 1000mu field mainly for laying hens feed. 75% of chemical fertilizer is applied while 25% is an organic fertilizer made from chicken manure. After harvesting, the maize is ground, processed, and added with some amino acids then fed to the laying hens which produce high-quality multi-nutrient eggs. The chicken manure from these laying hens is then processed through industrial fermentation, where acid treatment is done to reduce the ammonium and odor content. The end-product is an organic fertilizer that contains about 6%-8% N and this fertilizer is produced in both granular and powder forms. The fertilizer is applied back to the feed maize together with 75% of chemical fertilizer. The whole process is done to get rid of the ammonium gas emissions (greenhouse gas) which, as a result, protects the environment and reduces global warming. It is also a way of recycling organic manure through the production of clean and convenient organic fertilizer which is easy to handle over raw chicken manure.

As it was now winter wheat growing season, one day my colleague and I had a chance to tour around the fields on the proximal northern side of the experimental station. We, fortunately, found a combine harvester at work, harvesting maize on an approximately 12ha land. As it has been my wish to see how maize harvesting is done in China, this was a great opportunity to fulfill my wish. The combine harvester had a 5m head which was cutting the maize at about 0.5m from the ground and separating the cobs from the stalks. Just behind the head, it was mounted with another cutter bar which cuts the maize stalks into smaller sizes of about 5cm long and evenly spreads them onto the ground. The maize cobs were then directed to a large container after all the husks are taken off during the process. After completing each run, the maize was emptied into the small trucks which ferried it to the storage space for further drying. One interesting thing I have noted from this is the promotion of conservation agriculture (CA). 100% of the crop residues are returned as very small sizes which will not interfere with the planting and germination of the next crop. Furthermore, since water is scarce in NCP, the returned residues will also act as mulch which will further promote moisture conservation as well as weed suppression for the next crop. Some farmers were following the combine harvester and collecting the missed maize cobs and bagging them into sacks which minimized harvest losses.

World food security day—awareness campaign

China joined the whole world to commemorate World Food Security Day which aims to raise awareness on food security in the country by showcasing different agricultural systems that are enhancing food security in the country and the consequences of food insecurity among other mechanisms that ensure food security. It was also time when Chinese farmers celebrated their bumper harvest for the 2020 season. At 8:00 am, we accompanied Professor Hongyan and some other farmers to a nearby large-scale farmer field where combine harvesting of maize was showcased. Upon arrival, we started de-husking a land portion of maize where we took a sample for yield estimation. At the same time, 4 combine harvesters were busy making runs all over the field, harvesting maize in a very organized and fantastic way. 77 maize cobs were collected from a 12m² land area, 10 of which were shelled to represent the whole sample land and weighed. After weighing, moisture content was determined using a moisture meter to come up with an average of 31%. Data was collected and calculations were done using a constant moisture content of 14% which resulted in a yield per hectare of 12.2t. This high yield is quite common in China as it is enhanced by advanced mechanization, superb cropping systems, improved seed varieties, and adequate nutrient resources.

We also had an opportunity to meet with almost 1,000 junior students from different schools around Quzhou county who visited CAU experimental station accompanied by their teachers. The occasion started around 8:30 am when CAU through its Quzhou Experimental Station had joined the world to campaign World Food Day. The campaign was teaching junior students about how China transformed from famine into securing food for every citizen through the years. Many CAU staff were giving some speeches on this topic. We also had a wonderful opportunity to address the status of food security in our 8 African countries and also to mix up and mingle with them while having fun. It was a great day full of joy.

Our return to Beijing from Quzhou

It was the 23rd of November 2020 when we left Quzhou Experimental Station for Beijing after a long rural experience of almost 6 months. I woke up early in the morning and started packing up all my belongings. Before we left, the station workers together with us took a couple of pictures from around the experimental station which would create a lot of memories even to us during the wonderful time we had in Quzhou. The practical education training involved carrying out various practical work which includes conducting field experiments, practical training on China's agricultural technological advancement by the surrounding small-scale farmers, and class presentations.

Generally, the training program was such a fruitful experience as it gave the students much hands-on exposure to almost all practical aspects of agriculture in China as well as the experience in conducting field experiments. Many technologies and approaches used in solving farmers' problems were gained and I look forward to transferring them to my country, Zimbabwe, to sustainably improve farmers' yield and income. Much progress was also made in thesis research and development during this period.

My life in China, practical experience at Quzhou

Derara Sori Feyisa

My arrival in Beijing, China

It was on September 7, 2019 that I left my beloved ones and country Ethiopia in order to pursue my master's degree in China. It was my special day that I will never forget in my life. At that moment international flight was new for me and I was a little bit scared of flight since I was alone. Whatever it was, I arrived in Beijing at about 11:00 pm on the same day since my flight was nonstop.

Life in Quzhou Experimental Station

Moving to Quzhou was great joy since we were tired of always staying in the room due to Covid-19 and also we were eager to start practical education. When we finished class lecturs we moved to Experimental Station in order to start practical education that was planned by the university. It was on June 2, 2020 that we moved to Quzhou Experimental Station. We arrived at Quzhou Experimental Station at about 4:10 pm and were welcomed warmly by the staff. Quzhou Experimental Station is the best and safest place for study. In Quzhou you can have three things together: farming community, knowledge and communication. Since it is a place where you can find these three combined things, it was great opportunity to learn and gain experience based knowledge through practice. The next morning we started to visit the compound of the station in order to identify technologies which have been practiced in the station. Following this we observed all experiments and a brief explanation was given to us by Professor Jiao Xiaoqiang. In general during my stay in Quzhou I have learnt a lot through practice and observation. I was able to gain experience based knowledge through two ways: academic research and field observation.

Academic research

In Quzhou, for academic research, I have conducted household survey to evaluate technical efficiency of small scale wheat producer in Quzhou county. Regarding to household survey, my original plan was to interview around 120 sample farmers. But due to this pandemic issue I could not collect data as of my first plan. Besides COVID-19, language barrier is another factor that hindered me to collect sufficient data. If I were Mandarin speaker, I could collect data at any time independently. Since I had no person to help me regularly, I would not be able to collect my date as of my plan. I discussed with my supervisor who suggested me to collect data only from thirty farmers and analyze the result. Following this we went out three days and collected from thirty six farmers' with the help of a Quzhou Experimental Station staff and my Chinese friend. Finally I would like to thank my supervisor Professor Jiao Xiaoqiang for his wonderful support and my Chinese partner Miss Jiang Shan who helped me a lot for my research work. Really I appreciated the contribution they made for me.

Through observation/field visit

The purpose of going to Quzhou county was not only doing academic research but also visiting technologies which have been practiced by local farmers as well as other agricultural related companies and agricultural stakeholders. During my stay in Quzhou county I made different visitations to different STBs and other agricultural related companies. I can say all visits were very instructive and contributed a lot to my future journey. The following are some of my experiences during my stay in Quzhou Experimental Station.

Farmers field school visit

We departed from China Agricultural University at 9:30 am and arrived at 10 pm. As soon as we arrived we participated in Yuezhuang village stevia planting technology farmers field school opening ceremony. The event was organized by China Agricultural University. The surrounding farmers, China

Agricultural University professors, some of Science and Technology Backyard African students and Chinese master's students conducting their research in Quzhou Experimental Station participated in the ceremony. The event was started by the opening speech of Jiang Rongfeng, Director General of Quzhou Experimental Station and other scholars who were the participants of the ceremony. After the opening speech was made and technical advice were given to the farmers by participating professors, training on valuable components of research recommendation was given to the farmers by Quzhou Experimental Station team.

Welcoming Director of Hebei province foreigner affairs

On 9th of July, 2020, we welcomed director of Hebei province foreigner affairs. Before the guests arrived, we put the poster of some students on the road in order to introduce what we have done so far, setting the book of daily report that had been done by STB African students. The director of foreign affairs and his team came at around 12:00 o'clock and visited the station. The team visited the poster erected on the road and explanation was given to them by Professor Zhang Hongyan. After explanation had been made by Professor Zhang Hongyan, the director of foreign affairs gave the speech regarding the life and relationship of the countries. In his speech the director said that in light of Covid-19, China is helping and will help African countries in terms of human resources by sending special doctors and financial support too. Finally the director concluded his speech by wishing good life for us and as they strength the support they will provide for African countries.

Visiting mushroom farm company

July 13, 2020 was the day we visited mushroom farm company. Before mushroom farm visit we had the class lecture on the production status and advantages of mushroom production in China and in the world. After the class lecture had finished, we headed to mushroom farm to see how mushroom is cultivated. In our visit two mushroom bases were visited. The first mushroom base was of *Agaricus blazei* (Brazilian mushroom) which is native to Brazil and discovered in 1960. The other mushroom base was *Pleurotus eryngii*. From today's visit I experienced a lot. In my country Ethiopia mushroom production and consumption is not that much normal. Today when I saw the big farm that was purposely established for mushroom cultivation I was surprised and started to follow the professor who guided us in the farm and explained about the farm. At the beginning we visited the cultivation material used for mushroom production. Crop straw: such as corn, wheat, rice, and cotton. Livestock manure: cow dung, horse dung, chicken manure are cultivation materials used in the farm. Mushroom cultivation process includes raw material preparation, bagging, sterilization (121℃ for about 3 hours), cooling and inoculation. Mushroom management was also explained by the professor, and the temperature is controlled at 12-16℃ and the humidity is controlled at 80%-95% for management.

Maize harvest

On October 18, 2020 we visited farmers field covered with maize and ready for harvest. The purpose of the trip was to see the performance of the maize production and how mechanized technologies were used by farmers on farmer's field in collaboration with Quzhou Experimental Station. In order to know the yield potential of the crop we attempted to take sample from the field. The farm was about two hectare and two different varieties were planted separately on one hectare. From two hectare we took yield data and tried to calculate the obtained yield. From the calculation the first total yield was obtained ten tones per hectare and from the second one thirteen tones were obtained. It is very amazing to see this huge yield on farmer's field under farmers' practice. When we compare this yield with the yield achieved in Africa by smallholder farmers, it is the distance between earth and sky, implying that much effort is needed to maximize production output in Africa.

Middle school visit and teaching students

On October 22, 2020 we visited a middle school in order to teach students English. For this purpose I got up at 7:00 am and had breakfast before the trip. Twelve African STB master students were selected to go at school and provids teaching service. After we arrived there we took group photo with the school's English teacher. Then two African students with one Chinese English teacher started to discuss on what to teach and how to teach. The aim of the visitation was to motivate students to learn English and teach them some words. The day was very interesting and it was a good opportunity to learn from each other. I and one of my classmate by being with Chinese English teacher joined two classes and tried to teach students. The students were very interested in learning English and we really enjoyed the lesson. After the teaching activity was finished, the students gathered together and we sang together. Finally we African STB students and Chinese students played football and accomplished that day's program.

During my stay in Quzhou Experimental Station there was a unique thing that I experienced from Chinese people. Fortunately my supervisor was living with us in the experimental station since he is a coordinator of the program. Really I would like to appreciate his motivation in helping the students. He is an energetic and dynamic person. To be honest he inspired me to do many things with great motivation. He wants all students to study hard and work hard which is very ecouraging. In general, life in Quzhou Experimental Station was very interesting and I learned a lot. Finally I would like to thank Quzhou Experimental Station staff for their kind support and China government for the opportunity we are given in general. I hope the experience that we have been sharing will bring positive change on the income of subsistent African farmers and the issue of food insecurity challenging African continent.

Into the unknown: My China Experience

Priscilla Tijesuni Adisa

Beijing life: Arrival and registration

Being ambitious from my childhood, it has always been my dream to study and work abroad. Therefore, I went about taking steps I believe would help me to achieve my dream. Fast-forward to my undergraduate days, whenever I heard of my senior colleagues been offered admissions to study abroad, I am always overjoyed and motivated believing that soonest I will be the one standing in their shoes. In the penultimate year of my undergraduate study, the desire to start my post-graduate studies immediately after my bachelor degree was aroused in me, therefore I started interacting with my senior colleagues who were then studying abroad to obtain information regarding how to make successful applications.

In 2019, I made some applications and had my fair share of rejections. On 28th July, 2019, I received an email from China Agricultural University that I have been accepted for a Master's degree in Resource Utilization and Plant Protection. My joy knew no bounds as I read and shared the content of the email with my family members. Thereafter, I started taking steps for visa application and booking of my plane ticket.

I must confess that August was a busy month for me. I was on the road for most of the time. Occasionally, I had to board the night bus in order to make it in time to my destinations which sometimes were places I had never been to. I visited my school to obtain my academic transcript, conducted medical tests, had my documents notarized by a notary public and authenticated at the Ministry of Education and Ministry of Foreign affairs. Moreover, I made my online X1 (student) visa application. During this period, I also made some research about the Chinese way of life including food, religion, as well as rules and regulations, China Agricultural University and Science and Technology Backyard.

On the 8th September, 2019 at about 8:43 am, after a 16-hour flight from Nigeria, I arrived in Beijing. What drew my attention the most was that almost all I had to do from my arrival at the airport to my exit was automated. I was picked up from the airport by a friend which saved me from the stress of communicating in an unknown environment. We boarded a taxi and headed for China Agricultural University, West Campus. All through the journey, she gave me much needed information about life in China, particularly, life as a post-graduate student. It took us about an hour to arrive at the school. Upon arrival at the dormitory, I registered in my dormitory. To my surprise, I saw some of my country mates whom I met at the visa application center, which was a beautiful experience.

Subsequently, I went to shop for basic utensils and groceries at a nearby mall where I met some Chinese who helped me with directions and shopping. This gave me a positive impression of Chinese. I thought 'Oh! The Chinese must be friendly.' I must confess that I experienced some difficulty adjusting to time difference (China is seven hours ahead of my home country), so it was difficult for me to sleep early which ultimately led me to wake up late. Similarly, I had difficulty adjusting to Chinese meals and ways of eating, particularly, the use of chopsticks.

On the 9th September, I went to the main campus (east campus) to carry out some registration. Thereafter, I returned to west campus where I registered my campus card, got a SIM card and created a bank account. On 21st September, I attended an orientation program held for foreign students by international student office where we were intimated of rules and regulations governing our stay in China. Furthermore, detailed explanation was provided regarding the grading system, and requirements of each degree (Bachelors, Masters, Doctoral degrees).

Course work

Academic work for me started at the end of September. My course work was divided into general courses and department specific courses. The general courses were Research Integrity and Academic Norms as well as Elementary

Chinese. I enjoyed every bit of the Chinese from the written aspect to the oral aspect. I was able to acquire knowledge of basic vocabulary needed for day-to-day activities. The first word I learnt was 'Hello – Ni Hao'. Through the course I was able to learn several conversations needed when I visit supermarkets, restaurants and banks. It was an exciting experience for me. In addition, this Research Integrity and Academic Norms provided me with highly expository knowledge norms and misconduct in academic research which has been of great use to me in my current research.

The department specific courses were Integrated Management of Plant Pests, Thesis Writing in Plant Nutrition, Advanced Experimental Design and Biostatistics, Safe Production of Agro-Produce, Efficient Utilization and Management of Agrochemical Products, Agricultural Non-Point Source Pollution, Modern Agricultural Innovation and Rural Revitalization Strategy, and Advances in Resource Utilization and Plant Protection. These courses commonly highlighted the challenge we are faced with globally—feeding the rapidly increasing population in environmentally sustainable and socially sustainable ways. I was exposed to the implications of currently unsustainable agriculture that is currently being practiced on environmental health and this further increased in me the desire to be a change agent by promoting sustainable agriculture.

Quzhou experience: arrival and orientation

After more than three months of staying indoors as a result of the lockdown, and eight months of anticipating the move to Quzhou county, Hebei province, along with other Sino-Africa STB students I set out for Quzhou Experimental Station on 2nd June, 2020. The journey started from China Agricultural University, West Campus, Beijing at 9:15 am. The journey to Quzhou was an eye opener on agriculture in China. I got to see farmlands and other new places in China. The journey took about 6 hours and I arrived at Quzhou Experimental Station at 3:54 pm. The environment of the experimental station was homelike.

On 3rd June, 2020, I participated in the orientation walk where Dr. Jiao Xiaoqiang introduced to us (Sino-Africa STB students) the experimental station. The whole team visited ongoing field and greenhouse experiments and the workshop which housed tractors, sprayers, planters and combine harvesters among other equipments. It was the first time for me to see some of the equipments.

After the early visits to diverse STBs, I devoted most of my days to preparation for my proposal defense. I reviewed many literature while preparing my PowerPoint and Word documents. On June 26th, I had my proposal defense. It was nerve-racking at the start but after my presentation I was relieved as the defense committee made pleasant comments on my presentation and gave constructive criticisms and suggestions.

Research and hands-on experience

Due to the unavailability of seeds of soybean cultivars for my experiment, I was unable to conduct my research. Rather than staying idle, I conducted extensive literature review and acquired hands on experience on how my experiments would be conducted as well as bioinformatics analysis of my results during my stay at the experimental station.

My research is focused on strengthening protective rhizosphere microbiome for better plant nutrition. My crop of focus is soybean which is a main source of food for man and feed for animals. Although it is a crop of huge importance to man, its production is limited by pest and pathogens which cause an annual loss of more than 20%. The margin of loss is brought about by pathogens particularly *Phythopthora sojae*, the causative agent of *Phytophthora* root and stem rot and the need for development of environmentally sustainable ways of controlling the pathogen spurred in me an interest to conduct research on soybean root-associated microorganisms for the isolation of potential biocontrol agents. The isolation of beneficial microorganisms from soybean rhizosphere could bring us closer to the achievement of sustainability in controlling this highly devastating pathogen.

The hands-on experience I acquired during the course of my stay at the experimental station include: setting up greenhouse experiments, seed germination and planting, fertilizer application, assessment of plant physiological traits (root and shoot biomass as well as root traits), soil physicochemical analysis (available total nitrogen, available total phosphorus, gravimetric moisture content, total carbon, total potassium, pH and electrical conductivity), and rhizosphere soil sampling for DNA extraction among others. With regards to analytical tools, I acquired knowledge on the use of Quantitative Insights Into Microbial Ecology (QIIME) for bioinformatics, and R and Python programming languages for statistical analysis. All skills I acquired are relevant to my present research and future career.

Moreover, I took a course entitled Advanced Resource Utilization and Plant Protection. The course provided me with knowledge on the history and highlights of biological control in China, seed-borne disease and seed health testing, integrated pest control technology for organic agriculture, soil, fertilizer and water management practices in China. Summarily, the course emphasized the need for integrated management of agricultural resources for the enhancement of sustainability.

Seminars

In order to facilitate knowledge sharing among Sino-Africa STB students and check the progress of their individual research, seminars were held on weekly basis from July-August. The seminars were divided into three main parts, i.e., experimental progress, meta-analysis and literature review progress. Each presenter briefly explained the objectives and methodology of their research. Moreover, descriptive statistics and graphical presentations were used to summarize the results of data analysis. I participated in all the seminars and they were quite a learning experience for me.

Field trips

In addition to the research-focused skills acquired, I went on several field trips that gave me understanding of agriculture in North China Plain as well as scientist farmer involvement in agriculture for the enhancement of sustainability through Science and Technology Backyard (STB).

Wangzhuang STB

On June 6th, together with my colleagues I visited wheat fields in Wangzhuang village. According to the explanation of Professor Cui Zhenling, the lead researcher in charge of the field, farmers there were faced with difficulties in sowing maize after wheat harvest. Maize seeds are usually planted in the wheat straw returned to the field instead of the soil, and this hinders the germination of maize seeds. In order to solve this challenge, Professor Cui Zhenling's research group developed an improved spacing technology—4 dense rows and 1 blank row. 4 dense rows of wheat planted with an inter-row spacing of 10cm are followed by a 30cm blank row into which maize seeds are planted. The wheat variety used is high yielding (9.5-11 ton/ha) compared to the varieties used in Africa which have much lower yield. The field is managed via remote sensing technologies with drones monitoring crops for disease incidence and nutrient deficiency. A combine harvester was used for harvesting the grains after which the grains were bagged and weighed, and the moisture content was also assessed. Grain samples were then taken for nutritional content analysis.

After my first visit, I again visited Wangzhuang STB together with my colleagues on August 21st. I received exposure on why and how STBs are established as well as how solutions are provided to farmers' challenges. One of the master's students whose research is based in the STB explained that it was established in 2011 as a result of problems facing wheat-growing smallholders. Before its establishment, a survey on the smallholder farmers' agriculture as well as main challenges and the possible causes was conducted. Challenges highlighted by the farmers included poor seed germination, stunted crop growth, weed infestation, and lodging. Farmers, professors and students had discussions which led to research and development of potential solutions to the aforementioned challenges. Consequently, deep plowing and repression were used to combat low seed emergence rate, while improved crop varieties, plant spacing and weed management were used to combat lodging and weed infestation. Consequently, crop yields on farmers' fields were improved.

She further explained that after solutions were provided to the first set of problems encountered by the farmers from 2011-2014, a group of students and professors living in the village STB started deliberating on improving production efficiency, and found that an important constraint to increase productivity was land fragmentation. Cluster farming/joint production was suggested as a solution to this challenge. With this model, farmers are organized into groups; boundaries of close fields are removed; then, fields are cultivated and managed in groups but harvesting is carried out on individual basis. Although the land belongs to many farmers, there is much land that is suitable for mechanization, which led to the introduction of agricultural machineries of all kinds to aid mechanization of the whole production process. Moreover, full mechanized large-scale model of agricultural production was developed for the farmers. In this model, production cost is shared by the farmers while the STB provides necessary technical support. Farmers Field Schools (FFS), training, and field days were organized in order to help the other farmers without easy access to technologies. The farmers' leaders from each village are usually invited for this.

Furthermore, social media platforms such as WeChat are used to provide solutions to farmers' field problems. Farmers take pictures of plants with problems and send them to a group created for farmers, professors and students, where teachers and students recommend solutions. However, if the problem cannot be solved with the recommendations, a visit to the field is arranged.

Qianya STB

On 10th June, 21st and 25th August, 2020 I visited Qianya STB alongside my colleagues. According to our tour guides (post-graduate students conducting their research at the village), the village has a record grape cultivation. However, continuous grape monoculture, flood irrigation, and use of poor-quality manure led to a decreased productivity. Farmers grow a high yielding variety known as Jufeng, but it fetched low market prices due to poor quality. As a result of these problems and the production losses incurred, the lead farmer from the village, Mr. Long, approached China Agricultural University for scientific assistance.

In 2017, STB students came to the village to investigate the soils and did some surveys with the farmers. In 2018, an STB was then established, with a land renting capacity of 1.3mu. The STB students introduced new technologies like drip irrigation, fertigation, crop covering with nets, and bagging. STB students introduced new grape varieties to replace the poor quality and low profit variety that was being planted by the farmers (2 RMB/kg). These varieties were better in terms of yield and quality, hence higher market prices and great profits. In the new system, better management practices for the enhancement of soil health such as intercropping with strawberry, onion, and alfalfa were disseminated to farmers.

In 2019, the STB students collaborated with two farmers to build fertigation equipment. From their demonstration about 17% of water was saved through drip irrigation. Additionally, the management practices introduced provided adopters (farmers who adopted the innovations) with a minimum 700 RMB per mu. The demonstration fields were positioned beside the roads so that farmers can have easy access to the new technologies. Although, yield on farmers' fields and STB fields are equal, STB managed fields produce fruits of superior quality.

Dezhong STB

On 24th July, 2020, I visited Dezhong STB together with my colleague.

The journey from the experimental station to Dezhong STB took about 20 minutes. Upon arrival, Huang Hao and Li Zengyuan (the resident M.Sc. researchers) gave a comprehensive introduction of the station. According to the speech delivered and posters, the grape orchard was established in 2011 in Quzhou with just about 50mu land area. However, as time went on, the production faced challenges. These problems led to the establishment of the STB in April, 2018.

The STB was founded to enhance the development of this (Dezhong) vineyard. The scientific research approach includes farmer survey, field practice, summarized production issues, planting technology, Internet of Things sensor, soil testing, fertilizer formulation, and demonstration in greenhouse. The resident researchers further explained that the programme aims to develop a centralized cloud-based prediction station which is suitable for smallholder farms/farmers. This will encompass a weather station, field sensors, data store platform, and applications for analysis for decision-making standard system.

I viewed a quick demonstration of this computerized farming system which was displayed on the TV dashboard located in the conference room. After the presentation, the Chinese STB students led us around the greenhouses where grapes were cultivated and specific locations where sensors were implanted. In summary, it was a great time to learn new technologies. Moreover, it provided me with an opportunity to socialize with workers in a grape and wine tasting party organized by the hosts. What a memorable experience!

Visit to mushroom production facilities

On 13th July, 2020, together with my Sino-Africa STB colleagues, I visited two mushroom factories. Prior to our departure, Professor Zheng Suyue, an expert in mushroom cultivation and technology from Hebei Engineering University, was invited to deliver a lecture themed "The utilization of agriculture resources—mushroom". She gave a brief introduction of mushroom farming in China, and showed representative mushroom species in the class. Afterwards, we were led to two factories growing *Agaricus blazei* and *Pleurotus eryngii*.

The first mushroom farm we visited was Lixiang company, which was about 10km away from the station. The mushrooms were grown in growth chambers equipped with temperature, air and light sensors for optimum growth. The company used a mixture of biochar, cow dung and maize hull as substrate. The factory manager explained that the substrate used as beds can support up to 5 flushes (harvests).

The second factory produced *Pleurotus eryngii*. Although production was suspended due to the COVID-19 pandemic, I was able to see the production chain (Bed-log production, sterilization at 121℃ for 3 minutes, inoculation with *Pleurotus eryngii*, and cultivation at 20-25℃ for 40 days). Based on the explanation of the facility operators, the production process was cost effective and no waste was generated as raw materials were easily obtained and by-products from used substrate were returned back to the field as cheap alternative to inorganic fertilizers. The field trip gave me an exposure to mushroom production in China.

Using the methods as observed at the factories visited, China produces about 70% of the total mushroom cultivated in the world. The technology setup was regarded to be a cost-effective process by the operators. Perhaps because cultivation materials are easy to collect, the used substrates can be returned to farmlands as a cheap supplement for fertilization. Conclusively, the field trip exposed the African young scholars to sustainable cultivation procedures for mushroom as practiced in the Quzhou county.

Visit to Quzhou Historical Museum

A day to our departure from Quzhou county, I visited the historical museum with my colleagues. The museum presented rich cultural heritage of the county from sculptures (cooking furnace, animals, men and women dressed in traditional regalia, houses, horse riders, draught animals, wild animals), potteries, coins, farming equipments, paintings and instruments of warfare. It was a noteworthy experience for me.

I acknowledge all teaching and non-teaching staff of the university who at one point or an other have contributed to my success story: Academician Zhang Fusuo, Professors Jiang Rongfeng, Zhang Hongyan, Jiao Xiaoqiang and my amiable supervisor, Professor Song Chunxu, to mention a few. My study in China will hold a special point in the story of my life as I got to experience life outside my home country for the first time. I must say it is a blend of challenges and opportunities and I look forward to the great opportunities that my study would launch me into.

My trip to China

Coming to China was a big dream for me, because I have always wanted to come to China. I have always imagined how the country has been able to increase and develop in technology in such a short period of time, with its level of development and industrialization. Watching movies and documentaries of China gave me a perception of the people, which I was able to change my mind about some of them.

Coming to China was kind of a funny story for me, because when I was coming I was so excited that I did not make much enquiry of the weather. All I was concerned about was the fact that it snows in Beijing, because I have never experienced it, and it was something I was looking forward to, so I thought it was going to be very cold when I arrived China. When I got to Addis Ababa in Ethiopia for my exchange flight it was pretty cold, so I wore my jacket which I had in my bag. On getting to Beijing I realized the weather was very hot. I was so scared because I thought to myself that I was not in China, and if someone had told me at that moment that I was not in China I would have believed them. I later realized I made the mistake because it was still summer in Beijing when I arrived.

I arrived in Beijing in the evening, which was nice, because Beijing at night is beautiful, so beautiful, with all the lights and tall buildings, the roads, with all the signs, the beautiful cars and beautiful people... I did not want the taxi to stop driving. I felt like just riding all through the night, but we had to stop when I got to China Agricultural University.

China Agricultural University

I arrived at the gate of the university at about 8 pm, got off the taxi, and paid in Yuan, which was my first time to hold it. It felt strange because I had always been used to Naira for so long, and having to use another currency was amazing. At that time I was not even too concerned about the fact that language was going to be a barrier for me, because I knew most Chinese people don't speak English. All I had to do was show my admission letter, which I did to the security guards at the gate and they asked a student to direct me to the international building where I was to stay for the course of my program. On arrival I met some of my country mates who had arrived days before I did. They helped me settle in and showed me most of the things they have already learnt, like how to turn on the lights in the room, how the bathroom works and other things. It was an exciting experience for me. I also met other colleagues from different African countries, which was also amazing, because I have not had the chance to interact with other people from other African countries before. The first few weeks were amazing. I was still filled with excitement and disbelief. I could not believe I was truly in China, that I truly travelled more than 10km, that I was in a different time zone, getting to use WeChat, making new friends with both Chinese and Africans, even people from other countries, getting my tongue used to Chinese foods, using translation apps—which became the main means of communication, playing basketball in a new environment...

After doing all the necessary registrations, we started taking lectures, and the lectures were in English, which was cool, very cool. Most of the courses opened my mind to the extent that the Chinese people have improved their agriculture within 30 years, and the level of development and achievements was overwhelming, which was what I came here to learn under the umbrella of STB. STB is an effective approach to connect researchers/graduate students and farmers to identify key limiting factors, develop suitable site-specific DH (high yield and high efficiency) technologies, and help farmers adopt and implement DH technologies. The process involves firstly, to identify the problems encountered by farmers, secondly to study theories and identify the possible solutions, and thirdly, to do research with farmers to find the possible solutions.

My most memorable experience

Odigie Eromosele

My first ever snowfall

On the 29th of November 2019 at about 7 pm, on my way to the basketball gym, I was constantly checking my phone, because I had seen on the weather report that it was going to snow. I kept checking to know if the time was close, because I could not hold in my excitement—just the thought of seeing the snow for the first time was exciting me. At about 7:30 pm, I felt something cold drop on my head, but I was not sure what it was. I thought it was raining, so I tried walking fast so I wouldn't get wet. Only when I went to a streetlight did I see for the very first time the snow, my god! I could not contain my excitement; I put my hands out to catch some, wow! It was wonderful. I finally can tick seeing snow tick off my bucket list. I can never forget that day.

Class monitor

On the 5th of December, I was elected as the class representative, after giving my speech on what I hope and wish to do if given the chance to lead. It was a great honor for me to serve others, not just my country mates but my fellow brothers and sisters from other African countries. I really cherish that day because it really should show how much faith my colleagues have in me to represent them.

Won the college basketball competition

It was a memorable experience for me to be able to help my college to win their third men basketball competition, usually organized in October. I was invited to join them to play, and I must say it was great, because I was able to bring my experience and strength to the team, which was what we needed to win. My teammates were really fun and welcoming, who treated me with so much love and respect.

My Quzhou experience

The main aim of my practical education was to improve the researching skills and capacity for carrying out an experiment, which was achieved. We had a quick introduction to water resource management by Prof. Zhang Hongyan, in which he highlighted some of the major problems faced by farmers. Because of the low amount of rainfall in most parts of China, it was difficult for farmers to irrigate their farmlands. But some techniques have been created to reduce this problem. Some farmers who are close to rivers just have to get a pump to pump the water into their farmlands, Some are using other techniques like sprinkling irrigation and mulching, and those in greenhouse use some water culture systems, well irrigation and drip irrigation. This opens my mind to many ways to solve most of the water problems in Nigeria. After the course, I came to the understanding that one of the major problems in resource management in Nigeria is crude oil which Nigeria is very well known for. Nigeria's oil has come at the loss of its agriculture sector, and that is why the state of hardship is on the rise.

Nigeria's prevalence of food and nutrition poverty is attributed to a variety of reasons, including rapid urbanization, fast population growth, weak agricultural productivity, insufficient access to education and health care, inadequate availability of basic facilities, bad hygiene, sanitation, and restricted access to drinking water.

After my proposal defense, I started with the preparation for my experiment by exploring the internet and other scientific search engines like the web of sciences, Google scholar, research gate, to mention a few. I had to familiarise myself with all these tools to assist me to write my proposal and to guide me in my experiment. The title of my experiment is the Effect of Phosphorus Fertilizer on the Yield of Millet. I had to understand why it is important to carry out this experiment. According to Rebafka et al., 1993, in western Africa, millet is the most commonly produced and perhaps the most commonly eaten crop. Phosphorus deficiency is the biggest problem in the initial stages of millet production. Nutrient deficiency during the early growth and development of plants can reduce yield, as different yield controlling factor components are developed at this stage, and the best part of the country to grow millet in Nigeria is the northern zone, due to the low rainfall and dry weather conditions that favor millet production. However, the soil is mostly sandy, and according to Bationo and Mokwunye, 1991b, the fertility of the acid sandy soils in the Sahel zone depends primarily on the availability of P and the content of organic matter. Since the aim of coming to China to study is to improve myself and take the knowledge back to my country to improve food production, it was necessary to note that the rate at which phosphorus was mined—in the next hundreds of years it might not be readily available, so the need to efficiently use the P fertilizer is very important.

After much discussion with my supervisor, he had some concerns over my proposed experimental work, so he suggested to run a trial experiment, which I did. The pre-experiment was carried out in the greenhouse in Quzhou Experimental Station. 5 treatments with 4 replications, the treatments were 0, 30, 60, 90, 120. Every step of the experiment was studied properly and discussed with my supervisor to ensure a good result. At the start of the experiment 20 millet seedlings were planted per pot, and it was already obvious there was going to be a significant difference between the control and other treatments. The plant was reduced to 9 plants per pot after 2 weeks of planting. The watering of the plants was done after every 2 days. Depending on the moisture content of the soil, water can be added daily, so it was important to check on the experiment every day, taking note of every change, taking data from measurement of the plant weekly and applying cultural practice required for the cultivation of millet. The millet was harvested 32 days after planting—it did not grow to maturity, as the leaves started turning yellow and were shrinking when torched as a result of a nitrogen deficiency. My supervisor advised I harvest and I can still get the intended result as of when it is fully matured. I took the pots to the lab. Firstly I used scissors to cut the plant at the point where it touches the soil, after which the soil from the pot was poured out exposing the roots. Secondly, the roots were removed and put in a bag, the root-soil was collected too and put in a bag, and the rest of the soil was collected in marked bags. This was done for all the treatments. The leaves were dried in the oven and dried weight was measured. The soil collected, some were air-dried and the other samples were put in the fridge at $-20\,^{\circ}\text{C}$ and $+4\,^{\circ}\text{C}$. The roots were washed, placed in bags, and also stored in the fridge waiting for analysis. The data collected during the experiment was imputed in excel and I did statistical analysis on them: SPSS, T-test, and one way ANOVA was attained.

During my stay in the experimental station, I had the chance to visit other STB bases to have interaction with farmers, and other students carrying out their experiments too. My colleagues and I visited Dezhong Grape Ecological Park, in the south of Hujinkou village town, Quzhou county. We were met by some Chinese STB students who gave us a tour of the facility. The company's subordinate Dezhong grape planting cooperative was established in 2011 with a registered capital of 10 million Yuan. It has built a Dezhong Ecological Science Park, with a planting area of more than 300mu. Cultivation mode is double cross V-frame.

My life history in China

Tefera Merga

I am Tefera Merga from Ethiopia. I was born and raised in a small rural community in Southwest-central Ethiopia. I completed my early education in my native country including a BS in Plant Sciences from Mizan Tepi University in 2012. I am now a graduate student at China Agricultural University. I came to China on September 14, 2019 to continue my education in master of resource utilization and plant protection.

The STB program

This program (STB) was a very important program especially for Africa to improve the production and productivity of farmers, to transfer different technologies to farmers, and to prepare and use different types of organic fertilizer. I loved China before I came to China, that's why I know they are a hardworking people, and also have the ability to create different technologies.

So even if there were difficulties at beginning, after struggling with different things I finally adapted and started to live freely after a few months. In the first semester we took eight courses, such as: Elementary Chinese, Organic Farming Efficient Utilization of Agro Products, Nonpoint Source Pollution of Agriculture, Thesis Writing, Biometrics and Experimental Design, Rural Revitalization and Innovation and Research Integrity and Academic Norms. All those courses were organized in their orders and we continued our classes. In China, many professors were invited to teach us from different organizations, universities and different companies on different courses and even for one course. This was different from our country. The course was also supported by excursions which made the learning process very strong, easy to understand, memorable and fruitful. It was a very interesting and joyful study time that we spend during our course time. After we completed our classes on January 15th of 2020, we started to take a winter vacation of 2020. I planned to go back to Ethiopia during winter vacation, but due to COVID-19, I cancelled my trip and stayed in CAU. The Science and Technology Backyard program needs three consecutive years to complete: 1st year theoretical part in the class, 2nd year research in my own country, and last year back to China to write and defense. But due to the Covid-19 outbreak, we stayed here in China, for both the 1st and 2nd years.

Research plan: As for my research, I conducted my experimental research during summer on maize, in Luannan county, China, in Luannan STB, in pot maize production, on the title "Effect of liquid cattle manure on yield of maize and soil health." From 34 African STB students, we two me and my colleague went to Luannan STB. We left CAU, on May 21, 2020, with our advisor to Luannan STB. Our supervisor took us to Luannan and we stayed there for six months from late May to early November. During my stay in Luannan we did so many things.

One month after we arrived at Luannan county, we were became familiar with the environment and Luannan people inside and outside of the Science and Technology Backyard (STB). On June 11, 2020, we started our journey from Luannan STB at 1:00 am to Yutian county with our advisor Professor Zhang Weifeng to discuss our treatment with the manager of a fertilizer producing factory. We discussed all the things concerning our treatment especially about organic fertilizer which is very important and eco-friendly nowadays. We agreed with them on our issues and visited workers of the company, different fertilizers, different machines and equipments used in the factory. All of us were happy with our collaboration and we agreed to work together for more sustainability in agriculture.

On 12th June 2020, I got up at 5:00 am to identify our experimental site near Luannan STB. We started our journey with my roommate and my Chinese friends from Luannan STB in the northeast direction approximately five kilometers away from where we lived. We took soil samples and prepared for laboratory tests: the total nitrogen, total phosphorous, total potassium, available phosphorous, available potassium, cation exchange capacity, electric conductivity, soil pH, soil texture, bulk density and etc. In short, to test the soil physical property, chemical property and biological property.

During my stay in China I saw that Chinese government supports farmers' by supplying sufficient fertilizers, and adequate irrigation water to improve the income of their farmers. In China the government works for its people and supports farmers by supplying sufficient agricultural inputs like improved seed, fertilizers, different agronomic chemicals, pesticides, infrastructure like lights, roads (asphalt road in rural areas), and farm machinery.

I learnt many things from my practical education and acquired knowledge such as how to measure plant growth indicators, the critical period to take indicator samples for different crops, and to work hard to achieve my goal. I get a hardworking habit from Chinese farmers. They are punctual in their work and they respect foreigners. Now I am confident and fluent enough to do an experimental research and any practical work concerning my profession, by implementing the knowledge grasped during my practical work in Luannan STB with my colleague during my stay in STB. In short, practical work is memorable knowledge at any time. We came back to CAU after we finished the practical work in Luannan in early November and spent our time reading different literatures, analyzing our results and writing a daily work report at the end.

Filling the Void! My China Experience

Solomon Yokamo

Journey from Addis Ababa to China (Dream into Action!)

On 8th Sept 2019 at 1:00 am, one of my friends and I departed from Addis Ababa Bole International Airport. We didn't get the direct flight to Beijing and were obliged to take one-stop flight through Qatar airline. After five hours' flight, we arrived at Qatar airport and took a rest for more than five hours. When the gate opened for the next flight, we checked in and started our flight to Beijing, which took approximately 7 hours. It is monotonous and very tedious journey. On 9th Sept at 1:00 am, we arrived at Beijing international airport. But the big challenge was the time at which we arrived at Beijing, it was mid-night, and we didn't know the city and direction to our campus. We started discussing on the situation and decided to stay in the airport until morning and to leave at sunrise.

At 6:00 am, after we had completed the check-out process, we directly went to take a taxi. We called a taxi driver and showed a map of our college which CAU International Student Office (ISO) sent to us earlier before we came to China. The taxi driver spoke Chinese and showed us the translated messages in English. Then, we started our journey to the west campus. We arrived at the campus after one-hour drive. When we reached the reception of International Student Building, they gave us a dormitory, key and electric card, and showed us our room. This was the day that my dream came true and I started relishing life in China.

Adapting to climate vs. food!

Basically, the official registration date was on 9-10 Sept, 2019, and I registered on 10th Sept by going to east campus. Before starting the class, we stayed approximately one month by visiting the campus, city and other historical places with students. The climate was hot and comfortable and seemed the same as my country's climate condition. I easily adapted to the climate, social life and daily movements, but the problem for me during that time was food. I wasn't able to adapt to the food totally for more than three months. The food that I consumed when I was in Ethiopia was *Bursame*, *Chukame* and *Omolcho* with milk, *Injera* with *doro wot*, and some foods. But here, food and the feeding system were completely different; even handling chopsticks was a new challenge during that time. The common food in canteen were cooked rice, steamed bread, chicken, fish, pork, beef and many others. Nevertheless, I finally started eating many of them.

The Great Wall (The place that I always dreamed to visit)

During the Mid-Autumn Festival, we had a great unforgettable moment with some of our classmates to visit the Great Wall. The program was organized by Beijing International Christian Fellowship (BICF) for three days. We started our journey to Huairou district with all the visiting families and stayed within very comfortable hotels for two days. On the second day, we started hiking the mountain by visiting the Great Wall. This is a place that I always dreamed to visit. But, in the will of mighty, my dream came true and I got the chance to visit on that special day. It is the longest wall in the world as well as a place with a fantastic history of more than 2,500 years which extends more than 21,196.18 km (13,170.70 mi). It is not simply a wall built with stone by using human labour, but an integrated military defensive system with watchtowers for surveillance, fortresses for command posts and logistics, beacon towers for communications and others. We hiked up a mountain starting from the low altitude to the highest peak for a full day. It was really a heart blowing and unbelievable place. After we returned back to our hotel, we enjoyed time with all families by playing table tennis, pool, boating and visiting many other wonderful sites near the Great Wall. This moment was one of the most wonderful and unforgettable moments that I will never forget.

Theoretical learning in Beijing

The program was intended for three years by staying one year in China for theoretical learning followed by technical education on the general modern agronomic practices and STB models, for the second year in Africa and again for the 3rd year in China to write and finish the thesis work.

At the end of September, we formally started our theoretical lessons in Beijing. Totally, we had nine courses in the first semester such as integrated pest management, advanced experimental design and biostatistics, thesis writing standard of plant nutrition, safe agricultural production, efficient utilization and management of agrochemical products, agricultural non-point source pollution and ecological control, modern agricultural innovation and rural revitalization strategy, research integrity and academic norms and advances in resource utilization and plant protection technology and finally introductory Chinese. Each course was designed in good manner and lectured by the most well committed professors and invited lecturers from the beginning.

Each course has its pillar area and deeply highlights its objectives and goals. I experienced the efficient utilization of agricultural products and the modern agronomic practices that lift the Chinese agriculture ahead. For example, in IPM course, I experienced how to identify pests and diseases, and the treatment and control methods. In agricultural non-point source pollution course, I experienced how to efficiently use the chemical fertilizer and pesticides to reduce the pollution to protect our ecology from pollution. Also, in statistics and related courses I experienced how to develop proposal, how to find a research gap, design the field experiment, record data, analyze and report. During our stay, we had excursion around Beijing such as waste water recycling centre, the CAU long term experimental station including greenhouse and field experiment, the Olympic park, shared organic production farms and others. Also, I experienced on the organic production system, compost preparation, agricultural input management and a plethora of unmentioned activities.

The most exciting course was Introductory Chinese. It was given on every Saturday at 2:00 pm in east campus. Basically, I have a great interest in practicing two languages especially Chinese and French, but I had no chances before to learn. But now, my dream came true and I got the chance to learn Chinese. The lecturer professor Sui was very committed and taught us in a good way. The book was organized by sixteen chapters and we finished only twelve chapters due to time shortage, but I grasped many words and was able to write some Chinese characters. I became able to react and reply on the questions related with exchanging salutation, shopping, asking for help and others. At the end of the class, we had an exam, both writing and speaking exam and I never forget that moments especially the questions that my teacher asked me such as what is the time now, what is the day today, where are you from, what is your favourite food and others in Chinese. I replied almost all with poor pronunciation. Generally, this course opened a bright door for me to practice the Chinese language with high interest.

Journey from Beijing to Quzhou

On 2nd June 2020, we had started our journey from Beijing to Quzhou at 9:10 am. The college informed us of the whole program arrangements on each step earlier. After three hours journey, the driver stopped the bus in one town and we entered a beautiful hotel to have our lunch. After we had our lunch, Professor Jiao Xiaoqiang ordered us to quickly enter the bus and continue our journey. We arrived Quzhou Experimental Station at around 3:25 pm.

When we arrived at the station, Professor Rongfeng, Professor Hongyan, the Chinese students (Doctoral and Master students) such as GuoYu, Jiang Shan, Gong Haiqing, Guo Bin and other staff members in the station warmly welcomed us. The staff already arranged our dormitory and prepared a study room for each of us. After this, I took the dinning card (meal card) and meal box from the coordinators. I entered my dorm, took a hot shower and started breathing new air in the new environment. At 8:00 pm, our professors organized a meeting in the hall and presented us about the ethics of the station, rules and regulations of the experimental station as well as about abiding and keeping the community rules and briefly explained us our next work during our stay in the county, about seminar arrangements and meta-analysis works. My dream that I have been always striving for to learn something skillful which allows me to help farmers came true.

After I joined a new environment, the first things I conducted was visiting the entire compounds. Basically, the environment matters a lot. I visited the station a plethora of field experiments, greenhouse and pot experiments, farm machineries, laboratory, study room and many other places. I was very excited by seeing such activities in the station which opened a door to learn multidisciplinary knowledge and skills. But my worry was about food. There were not many choices in the canteen as compared with CAU (Beijing) and I totally felt uncomfortable, but through a time I adopted it and enjoyed everything in the canteen during my stay in Quzhou.

Proposal defence

After many efforts and tough work, my dream became absolutely true. That day and place was 25th Sept, 2020 in Quzhou Experimental Station. It was a historical day for me that I presented my proposal work. I presented my research proposal entitled "the effects of organic manure on growth and yield of maize and soil health". What a special day! I didn't have this kind of exposure before to present in front of many professors and academicians. Actually, the committee members (evaluators) were in Beijing, holding the meeting online. I started presenting my work for 15 minutes and our professors asked me very constructive and instructive questions that I would never forget and suggested me in a directive way. Some questions raised from evaluators and attendants were: What does "with organic equivalency of NPK" mean? What is the gap between your work and other researchers work? How do you classify different management systems of organic fertilizers in your meta-analysis work? And how are you going to group or arrange them? Then after wards, I replied some points and received some suggestions and comments to incorporate in my work and I finished my session in good way by thanking them. After all students finished presenting their proposals on 26th June, the committee member gave us a general comment and the director of our program Professor Jiang Rongfeng made a closing speech on two points by saying: "Every student should communicate and discuss with their respective supervisor to improve their work" and "use the same template/format for your proposal before submitting to final evaluation". This moment is a special time for me which provoked my motive to do better work then after.

Lecture class and visit to Quzhou Experimental Station Archive

On 8th June, 2020, we started a new course entitled "Advances in resource utilization and plant protection technology". The course was organized by Professor Zhang Hongyan. It was organized in a good manner and he overviewed the general objectives of the course and what the current

Chinese agriculture looks like and what challenges it faces. Through this course, I experienced many theoretical knowledge and practical skills. For example, the main problem of China's modern agriculture is low efficiency, the quality and quantity of food to meet the demand of consumers and different environmental problems such as eutrophication, acidification, soil salinization & pollution, leaching, water pollution and etc. Also, pest and disease are the main problems. Surprisingly, the course has two major tips to give a clue and solution to solve the aforementioned problems: efficient and effective resource utilization as the first tip and plant protection as another tip. When I saw the content of the course, I was really motivated to follow this course intensively because it is very interesting. Efficient use of agricultural inputs such as fertilizer, seed, water, pesticide, herbicide and others to solve the burgeoning agricultural problems and the mechanism of managing the crop production enemies such as pest, disease and weeds under field and storage areas for reducing the loss and ensuring food security sustainably were the general points that I kept in my mind.

At the end of the lecture class, we went to the archive of Quzhou Experimental Station. Really, it is a very amazing place with a dose of history throughout the time for many decades. You can find the history of Quzhou Experimental Station from the early establishment in 1973 up to date. Our Professor Zhang Hongyan have explained to us each step in the archive from the beginning: why the experimental station was established, how it was established, what was done before, what changes were recorded and what awards they won and what is taking place in and around the station... Inside the archive there was plenty of postures that shows the different research and community works conducted starting from 1973 and the photos that were taken of different scientists working together with farmers. That was a special day that aroused my interest in recording such a rare event.

Sino-Africa STB program seminars

Every Wednesday during our stay in Quzhou Experimental Station, the program coordinator Professor Jiao Xiaoqiang organized a mini-seminar for all students and 5-8 students presented their progress reports on field experiments, literature review, meta-analysis and other current topics. I was very lucky to present my works many times especially my meta-analysis research work. In the seminars, teachers ask the question and show a direction, while students ask any unclear points. It is really an interesting moment that built my confidence to speak in such scientific places, to improve my skill and work quality and to show constant progress for my work.

Field work in 300mu experimental base

I started conducting field experiment in 300mu experimental base outside the main station. The experiment consisted of two types of fertilizer (organic and mineral) at four different rates. The experiment was started in June and continued until October. My supervisor Professor Jiang Rongfeng, program coordinator Professor Jiao and my Chinese partner Mr. Li Yiming and Ms. Zhang Surui were helping me through technically and providing necessary equipments and advices to the success of the work. Before planting of the summer maize, pre-experiment soil sample was collected in Zigzag manner from the top 20cm layers and one representative sample was composited from the plot using soil-Auger (inner diameter 2cm) from the top 20cm layers. This soil was air dried at room temperature and then passed through a 0.25 mm mesh and analysed for available soil nutrients.

The maize was planted by applying all the relevant agronomic practices. When the plant reached the pre-planned data collection stages, I together with others African STB students and Chinese partners started collecting and recording relevant data. Totally, the agronomic data were collected five times throughout the plant growth stages. Conducting field work is not an easy task and requests thoroughgoing effort, time, strength and commitment. Most of the time I slept late around 2:00 am and woke up at 7:30 am. But, after I went to China, especially after I started conducting the field work, this trend was completely changed because of the time of follow-up and data collection mostly in early morning. Sometimes, you face a challenge when conducting your work. The challenge that I faced more during my field work was the language barrier. Basically, I know only the simple communication words like exchanging salutation, the languages you have used in canteen, supermarket or bus; but the language that farmers are using is quite difficult to understand. But, over time, I started understanding some words a little. Over time, the harvesting was conducted at the end of September and yield component data were collected for analysis. After we finished this work, we started lab work such as scanning root, plant nutrients analysis and soil test. In parallel with my work, I closely worked with other African and Chinese graduate students and participated in their work and acquired many skills and knowledge on the overall agronomic practices including field, pot and greenhouse experiments. Generally, I have learnt and grabbed interesting technical and practical skills on handling and managing field experiments from site selection, experimental design, fertilizer calculation, planting, data collection, harvesting, postharvest handling, lab analysis, data analysis and report writing. This work is a baseline for my future field work in Africa.

The visit to different STBs

It is supposed that Chinese agricultural technology best fits to modernize African subsistence agriculture. Science and Technology Background is the model that links farming and science community and other stakeholders together for mutual benefit in technology generation and dissemination. After I came to Quzhou, I have visited many STBs and coops and learned very astonishing technologies on different agricultural production systems. The Wangzhuang STB (this STB merely focused on winter wheat- summer maize) is the first STB we visited on 6th June, 2020 and our professors practically taught us about how to apply proper agronomic practices to achieve high yield-high efficiency on wheat. When we arrived at the demonstration station, many CAU professors (some of them gave us a course during our stay in Beijing), local farmers and some officials were there. The wheat field looked like the unrolling ocean and attacked the heart and attracted the eye. The crop already reached its harvesting stage and combiner (harvesting machine) was ready to harvest. The community people warmly welcomed us. The opening speech was done by Professor Jiang Rongfeng and other professors also gave us a brief description on what was done, about the technology and the mechanism of technology transfer to the end users. After the presentation, harvesting and threshing of wheat was undertaken and the yield was estimated. The calculated yield was 9.5t/ha. Getting this much yield is a miracle for us (African) and it was 280% and 164% higher than Eastern and Southern Africa average wheat yield respectively. This huge yield gap puts a big question on my mind "How possible is getting high yield in Africa as China has done?" that I will answer in near future. This day was very special for me because it was a day that I practically learnt the success and achievement of STB in China.

On 13th July, 2020, I joined a great event, a field visit on mushroom production. Before we departed from the station, the guest professor Zheng Suyue highlighted for us about the mushroom production and the share of China, the processing system, packaging and quality control. Actually, I know mushroom but it is not cultivated and rarely grown in fertile soil during high rainfall season in Ethiopia. We departed from the station at 9:35 am to the Lixiang Company and arrived after 30 minutes. In this company, we visited the input (manure, biochar, residue and others) preparation, mycelium usage, the bedding system, the watering system and the general management of mushroom. Here I was amazed that once the mushroom is planted (mycelium), it will be harvested at least five times continuously. After many discussions within this company, we moved to another site called 'Qiu County Minkang Fungus Industry Co. LTD'. This is a very big company but due to the outbreak of corona virus, the processing system was temporarily terminated. But we visited each and every step in the company, i.e., input manipulation room, processing room, sterilization room, packaging room and other steps. Generally, the team (Professor Zheng Suyue team) was organized and well prepared and they didn't hesitate to tell us the essential and interesting steps from production to packaging.

On 24th July, 2020, I joined another big event to visit the Dezhong STB. We started our journey from the experimental station to the Dezhong STB at 8:00 am and arrived after 20 minutes. When we arrived, the STB students warmly welcomed us. Two STB students started explaining about the aim and objectives of the STB, the general history, why it was established and what has been done after it was established and the research work going on in the STB. However, this STB mostly focuses on grape production system and varieties such as Victoria, Juxingyihao, Mixiang, to mention just a few. Here I was amazed at a plethora of processed foods and drinks by grape including wine and others. The other amazing part of this STB was the field management. The overall activities of the field and greenhouse system were controlled by digital system. For example, temperature, humidity, pressure, and soil moisture were controlled through implanted machine in the greenhouse and software developed for this purpose. Timing and rate of irrigation were controlled by digital means. I have enjoyed that day. Really, it was recorded as an interesting moment in my life.

The most beautiful event that I have enjoyed in Quzhou was the World Food Day on 16th Oct 2020 when the World Food Day and national food security promotion week of China were celebrated. The most interesting events were conducted in our experimental station together with the whole middle school students who came from the county, professors from CAU and other stakeholders. On this day, the school arranged a training and visit program in our research station for students. We explained to the students on the research work conducting in the field and greenhouse and also, we presented the posters on what the agricultural production looks like in Africa for the awareness of students. This is one of the best ways for the CAU to help young generation to engage in agriculture. Much more information was shared from different professors and I was really motivated to be part of this event.

Journey to Sanya, Hainan province, China

I have participated for some special workshops, meetings and seminars during my stay in China. But the conference that I participated in Sanya city in Hainan province was very interesting and special. On 26th Nov, 2020, I, with ZIGANI Saturnin and our Professor Jiao, headed for Beijing International Airport. We left the airport at 11:40 am and arrived in Sanya airport after three hours and forty minutes. The conference organizer warmly welcomed us and took us to the hotel. We arrived to the Mangrove International Hotel (the hotel that I had never ever seen of such quality and standard). The climate of Sanya seems my country's condition. It was very interesting and merely satisfied you. The program was the third annual conference on One Road One Belt, South-South cooperation, agricultural education, technology and innovation league (BRSSCAL). On 27th Nov, before the start of the meeting, we presented our banner on our achievements in China. From this program, I grasped multidisciplinary knowledge and skills. The conference mainly focused on the impact of Covid-19 on agricultural production and food security issues and its prospect through different scenarios and how countries adapted/tackled the problems, the collaboration and integration of the responsible stakeholders, issues related with technology innovation and transfer and cultivating experiences on multidisciplinary areas through academic presentation. Also, on the second day, we had field excursion to Yazhou Bay Science and Technology City (YZBSTC), and the compound looked like a paradise. In this city, we visited a molecular biology lab and learnt about how to get pest and disease resistant gene.

Generally, BRSSCAL is one of the best win-win cooperation which helps to share skills and knowledge, enhance multilateral technological cooperation, activate technology sharing and dissemination that aimed to solve deep-rooted agricultural production problems. Generally, I had a very interesting time to learn expertise from identified scholars and to know what the really existing situation looks like and how big efforts China is putting on African countries to meet food security. So, this event becomes the most unforgettable memory in my life because I contacted with many scholars and learnt broader concepts and unending knowledge.

Learning Expedition: My Experiences in an Agrarian-Rural Community in China

Lawal Olusola Lawal

Arrival at the Experimental Station

We arrived at the Quzhou Experimental Station on 2nd of June 2020. It took us a very long bus ride of over six hours from Beijing to our destination which would serve as our abode for the next couple of months. Throughout the first week at the experimental station, we were taken around in a familiarization tour of important on-going experimental fields and facilities such as laboratories, mechanical workshop, etc. It was a very revealing experience as we had opportunity to be exposed to the various top-notch and world-class agricultural machines and equipments at the engineering workshop, laboratory and greenhouse.

During the first week as well, we had the opportunity to have an interactive orientation session with some of the coordinators of our program where there were many important discussions concerning our living, activities and research plans in the experimental station.

From the second week till the 5th week at the station, we took class lectures of a new course titled "Advances in resource utilization and plant protection" by Prof. Zhang Hongyan. It was a very important and interesting course and we were lectured on various topics and latest agricultural development in the field of resource utilization and plant protection. During the time of taking this course, we also had the opportunity to go on field trips to facilities and industries relating to the course.

Practical field demonstrations

The stay in Quzhou Experimental Station over the last five months has been rewarding in the sense that it provided an ample avenue for me to gain many practical field experiences through the various field demonstration I have witnessed so far, example of which was the demonstration of wheat harvesting witnessed at Wangzhuang STB village. This was done seamlessly with the help of a powerful combine harvester. The combine harvester is an all-in-one harvesting machine that performs operations like: cutting, ripping, threshing and winnowing and at the same time discharging clean wheat grains at the end of the process. At the end of the harvesting by the combine harvester, grains discharged by the machine were bagged into small bags. The total weight and moisture content of the harvested grains were also taken. We all participated in all of these various operations. Prof. Cui Zhenling and Prof. Jiang Rongfeng were so efficient and clear in providing answers to our questions concerning wheat production and harvesting.

Wheat harvest demonstration

It was a great opportunity for most of us to have a field and hands-on practical experience on wheat cultivation, management and especially harvesting being done using a combine harvester. Apart from the fact that combine harvester provides a faster and easier way to harvest crop, it surely reduces losses due to hand harvesting and drudgery involved. At the end of the whole process, we recorded an impressive 9.4 t/ha harvest. This result had really improved our knowledge in wheat production and harvesting. It has indeed added to our background knowledge and it is a knowledge that will surely be beneficial to us.

Field trips and excursions

Another impactful learning experience during my stay at the Quzhou Experimental Station is the series of practical academic field trips and excursions. I had opportunities to travel out on many occasions for out-of-class practical trips to farms, agro-allied industries and agricultural resource facilities/infrastructures such as dams, irrigation channels and water gates in and around Quzhou county.

These outings provided a great opportunity for most of us to have a field and hands-on practical experience. The field trips also helped me particularly in improving my knowledge and sharpening my mind about many aspects of agriculture such as: water resource utilization and management, irrigation installation and management, and mushroom production using agricultural wastes. It provided an opportunity to have a firsthand experience of what was being taught in class. It was indeed a wonderful and inspiring moment to learn outside the class.

Farmers' survey

According to the nature and plan of my research/thesis topic (survey research), I am therefore required to carry out a farmers survey for me to write and complete my thesis. During my stay at the experimental station in Quzhou, I was able to carry out a farmers' survey for research titled "Assessment of challenges limiting the use of manure among smallholder famers in Quzhou county of China". A structured questionnaire which has been carefully translated into Chinese language was used to collect primary data from 120 participants who were randomly selected from two different STB villages (Wangzhuang and Fuzhuang) in the study area. The farmers' survey (data collection) was done with the support of Chinese partners attached to me by my supervisor, Professor Cui Zhenling. It was a revealing and learning experience for me being a practicing agricultural extension agent from Africa to have the opportunity to interact and carry out a survey among Chinese farmers considering the cultural and communication barriers.

It is interesting for me to note my meeting with the head of Wangzhuang village during one of my visits to the village for farmer's survey. He's a complete gentleman who is full of energy and very sweet personality. He also happens to be a farmer himself and after answering my questionnaire, he also helped me in encouraging some of his friends who are farmers to do same.

Finally, it is worth also mention that I have been able to improve on my field and laboratory experiment skills through the first hand opportunity I had in working and helping some of my African colleagues in their various field and greenhouse experiments/trials and laboratory tests. This has really helped build my capacities beyond an average agricultural extension agent into a nearly all round agricultural expert. I am very sure this will indeed have a positive impact on the discharge of my duties at my work place (Federal Ministry of Agriculture, Nigeria) and also in the transfer of sustainable agricultural skills and practice to local smallholder farmers in my country. The most precious moment during my six months stay in rural China was that I was able to interact and carry out a successful farmers survey among local Chinese farmers despite cultural and language barriers that exist.

Conclusively, I wish to sincerely use this medium to appreciate Prof. Jiang Rongfeng for this wonderful initiative of Sino-Africa STB program—this will indeed lead to many improvements and positive changes towards attaining food security and sustainable agricultural productivity in Africa. I also want to appreciate the Chinese government for this wonderful opportunity to study in China, China Agricultural University for providing an enabling and conducive environment for learning, and my amiable supervisor Prof. Cui Zhenling for his unrelenting academic support so far. Xie Xie!

My most wonderful discoveries in China

Philippe Yameogo

Introduction of my story

Known as one of powerful countries in agricultural field due to progress realized such as in the agricultural policy, agricultural innovations and agronomy researches, China is ranked among top producers of many crops (millet, maize and wheat) in the world. Thus Chinese agriculture development model is being admired by so many countries which consider it as an efficient model to fight against food insecurity. Burkina Faso, the country where I come from, does not remain on the side-lines of these thinking, and I as an agricultural extension agent was dreaming of deepening my knowledge in the agricultural field with new technologies in order to assist my country to build a strong agricultural system and in particular for small farmers to ensure food security. Looking for an opportunity, I fell on a China government scholarship giving me an opportunity to enter China Agricultural University through Science and Technology Backyard (STB) and that opened to me the road to China. Thus from 22 September 2019 I left Burkina Faso my dear country and my family to China, and at this moment a new life with many challenges was starting. My supervisor Professor Zhang Junling's wonderful welcome and her availability to guide me in my training have given me a tonus to stand up for all eventualities.

From Burkina Faso to China

After this success to the China Government Scholarship, the process to get the Chinese visa began. After a long waiting I got my visa and at this moment my trip to China became a reality. On 20th of September 2019, I left Burkina Faso for China. After around 20 hours of flight with stopovers around 45 minutes and 5 hours in Niger and Ethiopia respectively, I arrived at International Airport of Beijing.

My first days in China

Leaving the Beijing airport, my country mate Saturnin Zigani and I headed for China Agricultural University. That was my first night in China. The following day, the administration measures such the registration in my college and a Chinese mobile phone number were my first and urgent activities.

After a successful registration in my college, I met with my supervisor Professor Zhang Junling who assisted me in choosing my courses for the first year, and my study in China Agricultural University started. I was a graduate student of Science and Technology Backyard program in Resources Utilization and Plant Protection at the College of Environmental Science and Plant Protection.

During some free days without courses, I visited some beautiful places in Beijing town. I enjoyed this beautiful place called "Olympic Palace" where I enjoyed the mythic stadium called "Bird's Nest" that I used to see in the television during the Olympic Games held in China.

Theoretical training at China Agricultural University

Upon my arrival in China, I was enrolled at China Agricultural University as a graduate student in "Resource utilization and plant protection" in the Science and Technology Backyard (STB) program as part of the Sino-Africa collaboration for agricultural development in Africa. At this moment I was realizing that my dream was becoming a reality. China Agricultural University is one of the best agricultural universities in the world, the best place to acquire knowledge in agriculture field. There are 34 African students from 8 countries (8 students from Ethiopia, 9 from Nigeria, 6 from Tanzania, 3 from Senegal, 3 from Zimbabwe, 2 from Burkina Faso, 2 from Mozambique and 1 from Zambia). Many courses have been taught to us. Among these courses are:

- China elementary;
- Efficient utilization and management of agrochemical products;
- Agriculture non-point source pollution;
- Integrated and pest management;
- Advanced experimental design and biostatistics;
- Integrated management of plant pests;
- Research integrity and academic norm;
- Thesis writing in plant nutrition.

My knowledge in agriculture was only getting better through these theoretic courses and some excursions that I have attended at the university during the first semester. The quality of courses and the teachers' professionalism were increasingly stimulating my desire to learn more and to discover new things about agricultural technologies. History, principle and results of the innovative model STB were widely presented to us during our practical stage, and my desire to discover this STB was becoming more and more pressing. Thus after the first semester of theoretic courses at the University, 2nd June 2020 marked my departure from CAU east campus to Quzhou county.

From Beijing to Quzhou Experimental Station and my first days there

On 2nd June 2020 at around 9 am, we departed from Beijing to Quzhou county where the most important part of my training would be realized. After around 7 hours of travel, I was finally at Quzhou Experiment Station with my African friends accompanied by our coordinator Professor Jiao Xiaoqiang .

We arrived at Quzhou Experimental Station at about 4:00 pm. We went to visit the Yuezhuang Village Stevia rebaudiana planting technology Farmers Field School (FFS).The visit began with an exchange meeting with farmers at the Farmers Field School led by Chinese students from China Agricultural University, where the farmers warmly welcomed us. The meeting began with speeches given by Professor Jiang and Professor Zhang Hongyan. After the meeting and taking of some pictures with farmers, we were led to the farmers' fields where we discovered a new culture called *Stevia rebaudiana* (Burtoni) Hemsl. From Professor Jiang's explanations, we memorize that this crop is of great benefit especially for people suffering from sugar problems. Indeed this plant is rich in sugar but without energy unlike sugar cane. These leaves are the parts from which the main substance Polyglycoside is extracted after harvesting. The cycle of this crop is about 110 days and it can reach a height of about 1m. This plant goes a long way to increasing the income of farmers. In Africa, it is only growing in Zambia.

Back at the experimental station after some cleaning, and arrangement within the dormitories, and having our dinner, I participated in a general meeting started about 8:00 pm in the meeting room of the station. This meeting was opened by Professor Jiao and then, Professor Jiang gave a speech followed by Professor Hongyan. After the different speeches, Professor Jiao made a presentation. The aim of the meeting was to make everyone aware of safety management regulations of Quzhou Experimental Station, to present the summary of the activities and study methods that must take place during our stay in the experimental station. After Professor Jiao's presentation, some questions were formulated by students to clarify some points. Professors have shown their availability to lead us during our stay in Quzhou Experimental Station.

Visit and training in Science and Technology Backyard villages

In order to understand the principle and what was going on in STB villages, some excursions were organised. More than five STB villages were visited during my stay in Quzhou.

Visit and training at Wangzhuang STB: This allowed me to know wheat plant and for my first time to see wheat plant and participate in a wheat harvesting demonstration. I could see a large wheat field where a powerful harvesting machine had already harvested some wheat grains. I could also admire the high technology system used in the wheat production in this STB. I could memorize that this system is a new model technology to obtain a high yield and high grain quality. Indeed it is a system of rotation wheat–maize with machine utilization. Wheat is planted first with a spacing of 30cm between two rows and after wheat harvesting, maize is planted between wheat rows with a spacing of 60 cm between two rows of maize. The wheat is a Chinese variety called "Tongman 578" with high yield. I have just seen in real time the principle of STB "live in village with farmers, work with them in their own farm and bring to them new technologies".

The excursion during the course "Advances in Resources Utilization and Plants Protection Technology": After a rich teaching from Professor Zhang Hongyan, I learnt about STB and how to transfer it in my country. The excursion brought me a highlight on the irrigation system in agriculture production, in particularly on wheat and grape production in China. I could appreciate the connection system of the channels—the connection of the five rivers is very ingenious, very efficient system for water control. It was very surprising that to hear that North part of China consumes the water from the South part. The excursion led us visiting Beiyou village, where I also appreciated some fields irrigated by the underground water. My first discovey of grape production was in Qianya STB, where I appreciated the grape production with fertigation system led by Chinese STB students. This system is a new technology of grape irrigation to reduce water loss. Indeed, farmers use lots of water for grape irrigation, and this technology is implanted to teach farmer how to manage water. According to Professor Hongyan, the grape yield expected for this experimentation is about 37 t/ha. My understanding about the principle of STB system was increasing with each STB village visiting "Work closely with farmers, help them to diagnose their problems, and find sustainable solutions".

The delicious mushroom which I used to eat in the canteen when I had been in China was unknown to me, but the visit to the two mushroom manufactures, "Lixiang Company" and "Xiuxian Min Kang Jun Company" each specialised in the production of mushroom species *Agaricus Blazei* and *Pleurotus eryngui* respectively gave me a deeper knowledge on some different mushroom varieties and their production technics and now I could say something about mushroom. A plan of mushroom production in my country will be one of my projects. Seeing these two manufactures I understood why mushrooms are more consumed in China and how they are produced.

Visit and training in STB of grape production: My knowledge on some different varieties and taste of grapes have been acquired during the visit of Dezhong STB and Qianya STB. I could admire the taste of different wine made from different grape varieties which are grown in the greenhouse and fields. The more important thing I learnt was the technology of grape production (promotion of new varieties, fertigation system, etc.). My eyes were witnesses of the strength of STB to solve farmers' problems and to bring them some social assistance and also the interest that Chinese leaders have in STBs' work.

Visit and training at apple STB in Xianggongzhuang village: The visit to this STB allowed me to admire apple fruits in its trees for the first time, and the system of production and the technologies used have been largely known. These technologies without any doubt will be useful for my country in many fruits production especially for mangoes. What I memorized from the visit is that this STB has been introduced in this village at 2010 in order to improve apple production which adapts to soils and climate conditions of this village. At the beginning apple trees were big with low yield due to the density and the mismanagement. With the introduction of STB, big trees of apple were replaced by small trees. Integrated technics of soil management and pest controls were used to improve yield and fruits quality. Among integrated management, there were the use of reflexing film in order to reflex the sun light to fruits which induce good colour, the use of biology and physical control (radio sonorous and yellow trap) to fight against pest, the use of special bees for pollination, and the use of organic fertilizer coupled to soil cover by film plastic or straw to improve soil quality. The use of protection system of fruits using plastic or paper allows for best apples fruits quality. For the soil management a system of intercropping with grass is developed, thus grasses are incorporated in the soil eventually. All these technics allows to obtain a yield of 4,000kg/mu with best quality.

My experimentation on millet production

Millet, the second staple crop in my country Burkina Faso, is ranking among agricultural products with low yield. However, China is recording the higher millet yield in the world (2.5 t/ha in 2018). To understand technics of millet production in China in order to transfer these knowledge in my country to increase millet yield in farmers' fields, I conducted field and pot experimentations on millet production with the topic "Comparison of integrated nutrient management of millet production in China and Burkina Faso". The two experiments that I carried out (field experiment and pot experiment) focussed on the use of organic fertilizer combined to chemical fertilizer at different levels: two levels for organic fertilizer (zero dose and 5 t/ha) and three levels for chemical fertilizer (zero dose, low dose and optimum dose). The integrated nutrient management is the fundamental basis of my experiment because in my country Burkina Faso more than 70% of land are degraded and the low yield of crops in particular for the millet (853 kg/ha in 2018) is due to the soil infertility, low use of fertilizer and the poor management of soil fertility and fertilizers by the majority of farmers. Experiences which I have got during the implementation of my experiment are very valuable. First, for different types of millets, their morphology and their preference production zones are perfectly known through my literature research. Second, the production system of millet in China is not a secret for me, as the fertilization mode and the sowing system have been demonstrated to me with the help of a technician. The field management, the detection of some millet diseases and pest (downy mildew, ruts and millet stem borers), and also the different types of sampling (soil sampling, millet plants sampling and millet rhizosphere soil sampling) are known now. Third, the implementation of greenhouse experiment through pots has allowed me to understand all process for pot experiment. This pot experiment carried out in greenhouse was an opportunity for me to follow the development stages of millet and to diagnose the changes during these stages. The collection and data management of my experiments have been perfectly mastered with the assistance of my supervisor Professor Zhang Junling. During the implementation of the field experience, I got the assistance of Chinese people recruited as workers, the good ambiance of work and the collaboration with these workers were an opportunity for me to learn many Chinese words and improve my Chinese.

In the laboratory for my millet and soil sample management, I appreciate the help of Chinese students. Some students lent me their grinder to crush my millet samples, some of them their refrigerator to conserve my soil samples and others their oven to dry the millet biomass samples. I was really impressed by the kindness of these students. The manager of the laboratory was always available to our requests. I left Quzhou with great memory—I became very familiar with the experimental station that I did not want to leave this formidable training area. The great moments shared with technicians and farmers in my millet field will be a great memory for me. I will miss the fields, the laboratory, the greenhouse and the study room which were my work place. When will I come back again to Quzhou? This is the question I am asking myself. The memories will be forever etched in my mind.

Self-study and seminar participation

My days at Quzhou Experimental Station were noted by self-study session and the participation of seminars. The comfortable study room offers me a favourable condition to concentrate on my literature research and my daily writing. This situation of self-study has increasingly improved my capacity of reading, analysing and summarizing of scientific papers. The daily report with the aim to summarize my daily activities more than to improve my writing ability allows me to follow and to memorize all activities I have done. This has allowed me to be among awarded students on daily report during the month June. The term "grow together" or "learn from each other" found its efficiency during seminars organised every Wednesday. These seminars over and above improved my ability to conduct a talk in public, allowing me to acquire some knowledge from my classmates' experiments while improving my own experiment. Multiple talks with my supervisor Zhang Junling about my millet experimentation have changed in me the way to perceive scientific analysis. The availability of network connection facilitated my literature research for my thesis proposal writing and my meta-analysis.

Conclusion

My stay at Quzhou Experiment Station has transformed me into a new student. Apart from learning through my experiment on millet production, visits to experimental sites especially at STB levels, laboratory experiments and participation in various exchange seminars have forged in me a new person with a new vision on the agricultural field and the research level with more advanced analytical ability. All the knowledge acquired will be important for me to help my country to achieve sustainable agriculture and to fight against food insecurity.

Between the lines of a Mozambican student looking for solutions to Hunger

Teodósio Titos Leonardo Macuácua

Arrival in China and China Agricultural University (CAU)

In this first analysis, I will describe how my arrival and the first day in China went. On September 8, 2019, at 11 pm, my colleague and roommate Buana Suefo and I landed at Beijing Capital International Airport, whose goal was to fulfill the magnificent dream of studying for the master's degree outside of Mozambique, and I thank God to give us this opportunity.

When we arrived at the CAU, the taxi driver did not accept to take the money that we brought, because it was in dollars and he would only accept Yuan or payment via WeChat, but at that moment none of this did we have knowledge. For our luck a kind employee was leaving the gate, and he volunteered to help us and took us to the reception of the International Students Building, and we started to submit the documents for our registration.

On arrival, I was assigned to my room where I would live during my academic stay in China: Room 514.

An academic career at CAU

To ensure the success and compression of the process of establishing an STB unit in Africa, it was necessary to learn certain disciplines among which were plant nutrition, advanced experimental design and bio-statistics, safe production of agro products, efficient use and management of agrochemical products, integrated management of plant pests, non-polluting agricultural pollution, modern agricultural innovation, and rural revitalization strategy, research integrity and academic standards, advances in the use of resources and technologies of plant protection and elementary Chinese.

These courses which were taught by CAU professionals gave me a clear insight into the amazing technological advances that China had and continues to use to ensure food security. The classes were taught in an interactive way in which each student had to present on a particular topic and discussion between other students and the speaker was allowed. To improve the quickness understanding of the concepts, we were also taken on several tours around Beijing city, which included the Beijing Water Works, where water recycling is done, the CAU long-term experimental station where students and CAU tutors conduct their field and greenhouse experiments.

The journey from Beijing to Quzhou, Hebei Province

According to the plan of our SINO-Africa STB program, it was supposed that the second year (from July 2020 to June 2021) we would develop research or internships in our countries, but everything was changed due to the pandemic, because many countries have already banned the entry of international flights, many restrictive measures have been applied, to reduce the spread of the virus.

So on June 2, 2020, we moved from CAU, Beijing, to Quzhou Experimental Station, located in Hebei Province, where we would conduct our academic field experiments, as well as staying close to the farmers in China. When we arrived at the Quzhou Experimental Station, we were warmly welcomed by the station staff and other students. Rules and regulations were shared with us about our stay. Meal cards were provided to all of us for use in the canteen throughout our stay at the experimental station.

Constitution and operation of the Quzhou Experimental Station

The second day was planned to demonstrate the activities developed and operation of the entire Quzhou Experimental Station. The station is 70ha. Professor Jiao took the lead in making presentations, explaining what was going on, the goals and projects of the future about everything that was going on at the station, because, undoubtedly, this was the beginning of a long journey in the fulfillment of my mission as a master's student, in the search for the knowledge of the STB that will help us to seek research solutions, development and innovation in the production chain of various crops in my country for the competitiveness and sustainability of agriculture for the benefit of Mozambican society.

The first meeting was near the international building, then we walked towards the gate where we presented a team that was doing the wheat grinding, selecting the experimental samples of wheat, cutting the thorns, and packing in packages labeled according to the specific treatment for further analysis in the laboratory, such as moisture. After that, I visited the experimental fields or trials where the wheat and maize crops were planted and I was happy when I observed different researches in the field. Some experiments were done to compare organically with inorganic wheat grown in different parameters, such as nutrient content and quality, and grain yield. We then headed to the eastern side of the station where there were also some long-term experiments underway.

I was able to know that wheat is a food grain dominant in trade and that China is the second-largest wheat producer in the world, with approximately 130 million tones, a large part for human consumption. This crop develops well in cold climate. We visited a long-term experiment of the winter wheat and summer corn rotation system on its effect on the efficiency of yield and use of nutritional resources in the North China Plain. No notable evidence was noted in the performance of both cultures. However, the obvious prediction was that the rotation system could be a success in improving nutrient use efficiency as well as the yield of both crops.

After this stage of the field visit, we went to the machine park, i.e., mechanization area, to see several agricultural machines especially for the production of cereals: soil machine, irrigation machines, phytosanitary control, application of fertilizers, auto-mixed harvesting among other modern agricultural implements such as planters, combine harvesters, and plow tractors.

To understand the development of the entire productive chain it is important to integrate mechanization as an important part to increase the productivity of agricultural areas through the use of tools, implements, and tractors with adequate size and power that can help improve work time and efficiency. The other place visited was the north side of the experimental station, where there were fields of farmers and experiments of some students. A rare culture, especially in Africa, called Stevia was under cultivation. Stevia is used as a sweetener in tea and has nutritional value, especially for diabetic people. The crop was still in an early stage of growth and some farmers were doing manual weeding.

The last visit was to the high standard greenhouse where the experiments of some students were also underway. After enjoying the work around the station, I was fascinated no doubt by the success of agricultural production in China to guarantee the food security of the country. Agricultural research and development services are sound and managed efficiently, and all agricultural problems have been addressed. The Quzhou Experimental Station is undoubtedly playing a key role in ensuring that the problems faced by local farmers are resolved.

Visit of the wheatfield production in Wangzhuang

The day was planned by Professor Jiao for our departure for the STB demonstration in the village of Wangzhuang. The camp was under the supervision of the experimental station of Quzhou and this site has a prevailing moderate climate. The average annual temperature for Wangzhuang is 21° and there is about 277 mm of rain per year with an average humidity of 58%.

When we arrived we were introduced as students of the STB of Africa, and then Professor Rongfeng introduced us to some of the staff who informed us of the general state of the field and what needed to be done. In a total area of about 120mu (8ha), a variety of "Zhongmai 578" wheat was planted in October 2019 and the harvest only started on the day we arrived (June 6, 2020). The wheat harvesting process is considered extremely important, both to ensure the productivity of the crop and to ensure the final quality of the grain.

He then spoke of various treatments done there, such as fertilization, the spacing between crops, and the new planting model technology that follows a winter-summer crop rotation system. They use a highly efficient combine harvester equipped with GPS technology to measure the harvested area and other characteristics related to the field. This harvester has very minimal harvest losses. After the harvest, the wheat straw is returned and the minimum crop is applied for summer maize.

The wheat grains were of normal coloring, with brightness, without defects, free from diseases caused by fungal grains and bacteria without mechanical damage caused by the harvester. After that, the weighing phase came, and then the moisture measurement phase. Moisture is an important factor, since grains with a moisture rate below 13% can be stored for many years with little deterioration. The wheat was bagged in bags of 50kg, weighed and the moisture content determined utilizing a moisture meter. The average moisture content was 14.2%. The yield was then calculated and the variety proved to be unique as it produced a yield of 9.4 t/ha which was high enough in contrast to other local varieties with a yield 4-6 t/ha on average. The samples were then taken for further laboratory analysis of properties such as protein content.

The course of Advances in Resource Utilization and Plant Protection

The day was planned for the start of a new course (Advances in Resource Utilization and Plant Protection), which began at 8:30 am, and the same class was transmitted to other students who were not present in the classroom, through an online platform. The course was given by a teacher Hongyang Zhang who is the Deputy Director of the Quzhou Experimental Station.

In this course, the teacher explained to us clearly how much China suffered because of the lack of food to feed the large population. This among other reasons led to the creation of the Quzhou Experimental Station to carry out scientific research that helps farmers to solve their production problems by providing them with appropriate solutions and technologies.

After a detailed discussion by the teacher about how they could solve these problems, we moved to the historical building of Quzhou which was also inside the station, and there he taught us many stories of Quzhou and China in general. There were many photos displayed in the building that could easily help understand the historical events that occurred in those days in Quzhou and China. Since the establishment of the Quzhou Experimental Station in Handan district, huge yields have been recorded, the problem of saline soils has been solved, the incidence of the disease has been controlled and the degradation of land has also been reduced to a minimum, among other positive improvements. Since the beginning of the past decade, many students, mainly from China Agricultural University, have been trained there and many STBs have been established throughout China.

Water purifiers in Quzhou

The trips today were intended to show water resource management in Quzhou. The first point was almost 2 kilometers from the station and the second was in the Sanba Canal meaning Women's Canal, and the third point was Qianya STB (also known as STB grape). Professor Zhang Hongyan, started a class presenting the water routes that the farmers used in that area. In the first field, we found the following crops: beans, cotton, pepper, and trees. The producers used water pumps and nylon tubes near the canal. In the second stop, a water management facility where water flowed to different channels was controlled by five pipes. In this field, we found a greenhouse that was built with sheets of bamboo and plastic, and this technology allows the control of temperature and the reduction of pests and diseases.

During the explanation, you can see that China is a country with a scarcity of arable land, that is to say for agriculture. Of the limited land that exists, each farmer has no more than 1 ha, while on the other hand almost all or most of the farmers use flood irrigation, leading to much waste of water or no rational use of water resources, so it is necessary to know how to manage the finite water resource and combat waste.

Also, agriculture in China consumes much of the water resources which causes a reduction in water resources. China is one of the major producers of rice, wheat, maize, many subtropical fruit plants, and other crops.

Professor Zhang Hongyan spoke of three steps for waste water treatment: First, microbiological treatment. In this first phase, the wastewater reaches where the largest waste is filtered and separated. The wastewater undergoes a biological treatment, with bacteria that digest the existing organic matter. Second, treatment of solid waste. At this stage, the wastewater passes through the primary settling, where solid particles are eliminated by gravity, that is, they go down. Third, purification treatment. At this stage of treatment, wastewater is subjected to disinfection and nutrient removal. Remove bacteria, solids, and toxic compounds, making them cleaner. After undergoing this treatment, the water is transported through the pipes to the fields for irrigation purposes.

After observing this, we went to the field to observe a sprinkler system. The teacher qualified it as a good system, however it was very expensive for maintenance. Therefore, the use of plastic remains one of the most viable ways to control evapotranspiration, since the small producer can buy plastic, as it has a very low price. But it has a negative side to the environment due to its slow degradation in the soil.

Briefly what I learned is that water is one of the very scarce resources in Quzhou county, which makes it necessary to be efficiently managed to avoid unprecedented water losses. Many technologies are being implemented by farmers, which include plastic mulching, crop residue return, and other strategies mentioned to minimize water loss. Some of these measures I can implement in my country.

My stay in Quzhou allowed me to read a lot about the efficient use of nitrogen, because it constituted the central part of my research project. I visited several centers for the treatment and use of chicken manure. I dug deep into chicken manure, the main organic source of nitrogenous. In the progress of my reading, I learned that poultry manure is an important source of nutrients for crops in areas close to confined poultry production centers and can replace a significant part of the inorganic fertilizers used in these areas. To decide whether or not to buy such fertilizers, farmers need to know the agronomic efficiency of such fertilizers about mineral fertilizers, in addition to the price. The economic and agronomic efficiency of animal waste depends on its composition, the doses to be applied, the soil preparation system, the soil type, the plant species and the cost of transport to the crop, being directly associated with the number of nutrients present, mainly N, P and K, and their rate of release to plants.

Scientific popularization fair in Qianya STB and visit at the company Hebei Dade Zhiguang

In Qianya STB, a farmer was given the floor to give welcome notes and describe the event. We could not understand what was being said because most African students of Sino Africa STB do not understand the Chinese language. However, I was able to observe that it was the first campaign in the village of Qianya STB. On the table were 20 families of grapes harvested in the fields of the producers. The guests and students were invited to be judges of the grapes, assessing the color, appearance, and flavor of the grape, etc. According to the score and the awarded farmer will be the head of the Qianya STB plantation.

Several times we visited Wangzhuang STB and Hebei Dade Zhiguang Technology Co., Ltd, where we found several students among whom were masters. They welcomed us very well, explained the objectives and the work they were doing, and it was a pleasant exchange of experiences. In this place we saw several studies, works, and technologies of cutting-edge production, greenhouses with high technologies.

In conclusion, after participating in these events and visits, I realized that grape production is an activity that can provide a good economic return to producers, depending on the high production and prices obtained, but it is an activity that requiress high investment, a good level of technical knowledge about the culture, care from the field to the consumer since the table grape is a delicate and perishable product, obtaining high-quality products to meet consumer demand and obtain higher prices, among others.

On the other hand, for the success of Sino-Africa STB in my country, it would do so to connect the scientific community to the agricultural community to facilitate the exchange of information and innovations. Science-based management technologies are brought in by the STB team and discussed with leading farmers, the latter providing feedback that is then addressed, resulting in recommendations applicable to the holding. However, this requires large investments and government support from research companies and experimental stations in China. This led me to a reflection of the policies of Mozambique—in a way they need some profound changes if we need development in the agricultural sector.

Conclusion

After these fruitful experiences that gave me much practical exposure to almost every practical aspect of agriculture in China, as well as experience in field experiments, I feel that I must lead technological innovation and transfer knowledge to train small farmers and transfer the experience from China to

Africa, and that it is my responsibility to ensure adequate food production and conserve natural resources by reducing poverty through the development of the entire food chain. Many technologies and approaches have been obtained to address the problems of farmers and the environment, and I look forward to my transfer to my country Mozambique to improve the productivity and income of farmers sustainably.

I conclude by thanking the dedication, patience, and support of the CAU professors, administrations of the China Agricultural University, and collaborators especially my supervising teacher Zhang Ying who directly or indirectly made this experience possible as the pioneer of Africa STB 2019.

Exquisite tale of my life in China

Igbinedion Rosemary Izehiuwa

Arrival in China

On the 5th of September 2019, I departed from Nigeria—my home country for China to pursue a master's degree. I consider it an opportunity that needed to be seized and utilized. Agriculture remains the crucial focal point and sector in all countries and my country is no exception, So there is a need to improve agriculture in my country. With China being the second-best in technology, this is a golden opportunity to improve agriculture in Nigeria. I arrived in Beijing, China on the 7th of September 2019 at Beijing Airport. It was a pleasant flight and the taxi driver who drove me down to the school was nice. I loved the buildings and infrastructures that were in place while on transit. I arrived at the international student dormitory past 7:00 pm. I was documented and assigned to a room. On my way I saw other students from various countries in Africa.

Academic life in CAU

My academic experience was a great one. I was assigned to a supervisor by the name Associate Professor Huang Chengdong. My course outline included Advances in resource utilization and plant protection technology, Primary Chinese, Scientific Integrity and Academic Standards, Modern agricultural innovation and rural revitalization strategy, Pollution and ecological management of agricultural sources, modern technology and application of agricultural product safety production, Pollution and ecological management of agricultural sources, Advanced experimental design and biostatistics. I heartily enjoyed each lecture and the manners at which each lecturer taught his or her course. At the end of each course I gave a presentation on the course.

Primary Chinese was an interesting course as I got to acquire basic Chinese language for easy communication with friends and at the market place. In summary, I had a pleasant semester.

Arrival at Quzhou Experimental Station

Science and Technology Backyard (STB) is a program based on more than 10 years' practices in China. It has demonstrated considerable success in increasing crop production with high resource use efficiency, while also empowering smallholder farmers. The African STB program was established with the objectives of developing technology innovation and knowledge transfer in rural area with the STB model and to empower smallholder farmers in Africa.

On the 2nd of June 2020, I embarked on a road trip to China Agricultural University Experimental Station which is located in Hebei Province. It was a six-hour trip. On arrival we were welcomed and assigned to our various rooms where I settled in properly after my cleanup. At about 7:00 pm I attended a meeting organized by Professor Jiao Xiaoqiang. In his speech he welcomed everyone present and read the rules of the station. Professor Jiang Rongfeng welcomed everyone and spoke about the achievement of the STB program and its recognition and impact on the rural farm. He spoke about the activities lined up during our stay at the station and assured everyone of a pleasant stay in STB Quzhou Experimental Station.

Tour around the experimental station

On June 3, 2020, I woke up excited and energetic for the day activities. We took a tour around the experimental station. At the entrance of the station, I saw workers sorting, shelling, and bagging winter wheat according to the specific treatment applied for analysis. The experiment which was comparing the effect of Nitrogen and Phosphorus application proved that both elements are essential for the crop, in this case, wheat. The plot that had phosphorus treatment had many spikes on it, while the plot with Nitrogen treatment showed delayed maturity and low spikes. I also visited the long-term experiment field on winter-wheat summer-maize rotation system for high yield and high resources use efficiency in North China. The winter wheat-summer maize cropping system is the most common in the North China Plain. Winter wheat is planted at the beginning of October and harvested in early June after which maize is planted. We visited the agricultural machinery workshop where the machines were kept: advanced modern tractors, planters, and combine harvester. The combine harvester is used in the field to make planting easier for the farmers. The greenhouse was not left out—there I saw some students carrying out their research. The tour around the premises came to an end and I was back to my dorm.

On June 5, 2020, we visited Wangzhuang farm which belongs to Mr. Ho Ming for a demonstration of the wheat harvest. The variety planted was Zhongmai 578, at a spacing of 30cm by 30cm. A new model was used on Mr. Ho Ming's farm in order to achieve high yield and low harvest loss, the method of irrigation was flooding, the right fertilizer and application rate were used, the proper agronomic practice was done and the right harvester was used. After harvesting the wheat using a harvester machine, the wheat was poured into bags and weighed after which the moisture content was taken using a moisture content meter—the moisture content of the wheat was 14%. The yield estimation was 9 tonnes per hectare. This is an impressive result.

Proposal defense

On June 26, 2020, I was geared up for my proposal defense. My colleagues made their defenses, questiones were asked for easy assimilation of each proposal by the team in Beijing after corrections, and suggestions were given to each presenter. At about 2:00 pm I made my proposal defense with the topic on Nitrogen Use Efficiency and Yield of Maize as Influenced by Nitrogen Fertilizer Application in Africa and China. Few minutes into my presentation I had challenges with the network connection and I lost the team from Beijing but I managed to finish my presentation. At about 6:00 pm we went for a meeting which was summoned by Professor Jiao who would guide us on the next step to take in regards to our proposal and how to effect the correction made by the panelists. Overall, the day was a success for all the students, even though on a personal level it did not go as I had anticipated. My focus now was to improve my work and see to it that my field experiment was a success.

Lectures and field visitation

On the 8th of June 2020, at about 8:35 am we had a lecture by Professor Zhang Hongyan on Advances in Resource Utilization and Plant Protection Technology. He introduced to us the history of Quzhou county. He linked the several agricultural problems that farmers were facing in the past and how STB came into existence. The lecture ended after a long period of intensive discussions and interactions with the students. We went to the exhibition center which was located in the experimental station, and the professor took his time to explain in detail about Quzhou county. I had the opportunity to see the model of the houses and villages in an STB area. There were books, charts, and televisions that were used to describe the history and how STB transformed from inception. What I learnt and saw from Professor Zhang's class proved to me that a lot of hard work, research, and dedication was put into STB and for China to be self-sufficient in terms of food production. We also had a lecture on pest and plant protection, seed-borne disease and seed health testing by Dr. Laxin Luo, and we also had a lecture on water management and a field visitation to the various farms and where irrigation system was practiced.

The first farm visited was just a few kilometers from the school using the River Fuyang for irrigation on intercropping of beans and pepper. The second farm had farmers using water from a network of rivers which was named the mother river for irrigation. It was easy for farmers to access water in this region because their farms were close to the river, due to which they had a high yield and quality crops. The third farm visited used a well water irrigation system, and they practiced straw mulching according to the lecture given by Professor Hongyan. Straw mulching reduces soil water evaporation and increases soil organic matter. The fourth farm visited was a vegetable farm where cabbage, maize, garden eggplant were planted. The vegetables were big and had good quality and texture. We also visited a construction site which had a man-made river. Despite the numerous river and closeness of the river to some of the farms, farmers still find it hard to have access to water, and as such water shortage remains a problem in China. Farmers in the North China Plain get their sources of water from the South China Plain.

STB visitations

We visited the Qianya STB where the drip irrigation system was practiced. There I saw STB students who were carrying out a field experiment comparing the drip irrigation system which was the STB system of irrigation and the flooding irrigation system which was the farmer's way of irrigating their crops. From the experiment, I could deduce that the drip irrigation system was a better practice as it utilizes the water use efficiency for planting. I noticed some of the farmer's lands had burial grounds on them which makes it difficult for tractors to plow the land. China is facing a serious problem of water shortage. Some of the farmers pay as low as five Yuan to as high as 60 Yuan for irrigation of farms depending on the number of times irrigation would be carried out on the farm. Some of the farmers pay for only electricity while others pay for both electricity and the water used for irrigation. The second lesson learned was that farmers need to know how to apply the right quantity of water on the crop and avoid excessive water which becomes wastage because the plant needs a required amount of water to absorb and use for plant growth, as such water use efficiency is important for farmers to practice.

On September 29, 2020, I visited Baizhai STB for a briefing on the production measurement of corn for 1,000 mu of laying hens and the construction of branded eggs. The farmers were already gathered at the venue. It was a core demonstration base of forage maize at the 1,000 mu. The variety planted were Qiule 368 and Yuqing 358. The main technical points of the demonstration were: firstly, to detect new forage maize varieties with a high content of colloid and heavy content of pigment; secondly, to implement green pest control technology; and thirdly, to adopt the four unified management model. The model aimed at the low quality of feed corn, high feed dosage, low utilization rate, and low resource recycling utilization rate. The technical test was to form a green production technology of integrated breeding cycle to improve the level of standardization and green production of laying hens resource recycling and improvement of comprehensive benefit.

The method of management is unique and it is a recycling process. First, the maize variety is planted after which it is given to the hen as a source of feed, and the hen eats the maize variety which has a high nutrient content thereby producing quality egg after which they pass out feces which is then processed and used as fertilizer and treated properly to reduce air pollution and create a friendly atmosphere. The fertilizer is then applied back to the farm where the maize would be planted. The cycle goes on again. The farmer is happy and business becomes profitable which is the dream of every farmer. After the demonstration we visited the poultry farm where the layers lay up to 21,000 eggs a day. I must say poultry is a good business and a profitable one if managed properly. Some of the ingredients used in making the layer feed included corn, soybean extract, soybean oil, vitamins, premix, etc. We also visited other STBs, such as the Xianggongzhuang Apple STB and Wangzhuang STB village.

Field experiment

The major aim of my trip to the Quzhou Experimental Station was to carry out my field research, on Nitrogen Use Efficiency and Yield of Maize as Influenced by Nitrogen Fertilizer Application in Africa and China. Nitrogen is a vital plant nutrient and a major yield-determining factor required for maize production. It is very essential for plant growth and makes up 4 percent of dry matter of the plants. Nitrogen is a component of protein and nucleic acids and when Nitrogen is sub-optimal, growth is reduced. Its availability in sufficient quantity throughout the growing season is essential for optimum maize growth. Nitrogen use efficiency (NUE) is a critically important concept in the evaluation of crop production systems. It can be greatly impacted by fertilizer management as well as soil and plant water management. The objective of nutrient use is to increase the overall performance of cropping systems by providing economically optimum nourishment to the crop while minimizing nutrient losses from the field. While China is faced with the issue of over-application of fertilizer resulting in eutrophication, climate change, and smog, Africa is faced with the issue of low or no usage of fertilizer thereby resulting in low yield.

On the 13th of June 2020, the site area for my experiment was cleared and plowed, after which soil samples were taken using an S shape randomized method at a depth of 0-20cm using an auger. A total of 16 plots each measuring 6m by 3m were demarcated and ridges were made around them. The maize seed planted was Denghai 605 at a row spacing of 60cm, plant spacing of 21.5 cm, and a depth of 10cm. Fertilizer was to be applied after the emergence. On the 14th of June, the samples of soil from the field were air-dried in the greenhouse for three days after which the dried soils were ground using a rolling pin and 2mm sieve to remove debris and dirt from the soil. On June 19, 2020, I visited my field and noticed the first maize leaf had emerged. I had to make preparation and calculation of the amount of fertilizer to be used on the field. Four treatments were used for this research and replicated four times— total plots of sixteen were measured using a spacing of 6cm by 3cm with 5 rows in each plot. Fertilizers applied to the plot were urea as a source of nitrogen, single superphosphate as a source of phosphorus, and potassium chloride as a source of potassium. Application of treatment on each plot was carried out using a fabricated machine at 5-10 cm away from the plant. The method of fertilizer application was furrow.

The field was irrigated to field capacity two days after fertilizer application.

On the July 6, 2020, I visited my field and also replanted. The plot was sprayed with imidazole nicotinic acid imazapic as an herbicide on the 3rd of July which dried up the weeds, leaving space for the maize plant to grow. I watched my plants grow and waited eagerly to take the first parameter results which included plant height and the total number of leaves. The 19th day of July 2020 was the most important day for my field experiment as the maize plant was at the growth stage. I picked up the materials for collecting the data which included carpenter tape, a pen, and my record sheet. From each plot 5 plants were selected at random, from the 3 middle rows out of the total 5 rows.

On each plant, the following parameters were carried out: plant height which was done using a carpenter tape, and the total numbers of leaves which were counted through visual aid. The next data collected was at VT stage, and parameters included plant height, leaf area, SPAD, the total number of leaves, and biomass above ground level. Three plants were randomly selected from each plot, a carpenter measuring tape, SPAD meter was used in taking the data, leaf area was measured using a carpenter tape by measuring the leaf length from the collar to the tip and the width was measured from the broadest part of the leaf surface, the height of the plant was taken above the ground to the tip of the highest tassel, and a soil plant analysis development machine (SPAD 502) was used in taking the readings of the leaves. Chlorophyll is the green pigment that allows plants to photosynthesize. This process uses sunlight to convert carbon dioxide and water into the building blocks of plants. Because nitrogen is a part of chlorophyll, by measuring chlorophyll, one can indirectly measure the amount of nitrogen in the plant. This allows for more efficient scheduling of fertilizer applications. Three plants were randomly selected from the middle row, the heights being measured using a carpenter tape, the numbers of leaves being counted through visual aid. The height varied from 191.5cm to 236 cm, the number of leaves were between 10-14, SPAD reading was taken three times and the average of the three readings was recorded which ranged from 57 to 67. At the end of the field data collection, the leaves and stem from the three plants taken from the middle row of each plot were chopped and bagged then placed in the oven for 3 days at 75 degrees. I inputted all the data collected into my laptop for easy analysis. The whole task took about 2 hours to finish.

My stay at Quzhou has been of great benefit and impact. I have learned some improved agronomic practices and ways in which smallholder farmers can improve their yield. I researched literature relating to my thesis during my leisure period when I was not on the field or having lectures. My most memorable day in Quzhou was when I finally harvested my maize field. These experiences gathered during the course of my research was very remarkable for me. I learnt how the SPAD meter works and the importance of SPAD reading, and I learnt how to take soil sample using the auger with the help of my Chinese partner namely Zhenya and Guohao. I watched smallholder farmers using fabricated machines to apply fertilizer, to plant millet, and also to transplant. My field experiment came to an end 13th October 2020. The parameters were plants height, biomass, yield components such as length of cob, the diameter of cob, bald tip length, number of rows per cob, number of grains per cob, and total yield and biomass. The measurement of yield was taken for each treatment at an area of a 5.4-meter square and weighed. After weighing the yield, five samples were selected randomly from the total yield and weighed. The five samples were used in collecting the yield component of the maize from each plot. Three maize plants were also harvested for biomass at the end of the harvest. All the samples were oven-dried at 75 degrees and weighed. The result gotten from the five cobs varied between 1.68kg to 2.00kg while in terms of yield gotten from the 5.4-meter square varied from 7.72kg to 10.40kg from each plot. The diameter of each cob from each plot varied from 17-19cm, and the cob rows varied between 16-20. I had a stressful day at the field but as a farmer, I would say I had a beautiful day seeing my harvest. The cobs of my maize were so big and beautiful. At past six in the evening I took a walk around the station and noticed most of the farmers had planted wheat immediately after harvesting the maize. I also noticed they practiced straws mulching and mixing it with the soil before planting, which is a good practice. The winter wheat-summer corn cropping system is the most common in the North Chain Plain. Winter wheat is planted at the beginning of October and harvested in early June after which maize is planted and harvested in October.

Departure from Quzhou

November 23, 2020, we departed from Quzhou Experimental Station for Beijing. My six months in Quzhou had come to an end and I also completed my research. I enjoyed every field trip and field visitation we embarked on and the practical knowledge gained during the course of my stay in Quzhou. I woke up excited because I felt fulfilled that my major aim of coming to the station had been actualized. We took several group photos with the staff and workers of Quzhou. It was a beautiful moment for me that I was going back to Beijing.

The ultimate Chinese experience—agriculture, language and friendship

Theobard Stephano Chagga

One may ask me why not just do masters in Tanzania. The reason is that at higher studies the quality of education is very poor and there are not adequate facilities and funding to carry out research work in most of the universities of Tanzania. On the contrary, China has a lot of top ranked agriculture universities. And one more attraction to this scenario is Chinese government scholarship for citizens of third world countries like Tanzania who cannot afford expensive education in China. Other reasons are my passion to get more educated and serve humanity by doing research work in the field of agriculture. China as a country is also iconic to me due to the bilateral relations it has with Tanzania. The fact that China is promoting education and agriculture with Tanzania makes it a comfortable destination to pursue a Master degree in plant protection and environmental sciences. In addition, also of great interest to me is China's diverse, vibrant and well-preserved culture.

Arriving at CAU west campus opened up entirely new experiences as it was so fitting experiencing the way high level education works in China. We had excellent professors who dedicated all the necessary resources to improve our knowledge. I appreciate the fact that we got the opportunity to visit and work with modern laboratory equipment at CAU west campus, and that the excursions on organic farming just outside of Beijing were very informative and will not be forgotten. Also important is that, our stay in CAU west campus helped us to explore the normal life of people in a big city of Beijing, which gives us a perspective of Chinese culture transformation from ancient times that we read in literature to the modern day that we can now experience for ourselves. All in all, it has been a rather enjoyable experience exploring all that we could during our stay in Beijing and that being said, massive appreciation to the CAU staff and all individuals who were involved in making our stay smooth and enjoyable.

Eeperiences in Quzhou Experimental Station

June 2, 2020 marks our first trip to Quzhou Experimental Station in Hebei province. Quzhou is a designated base for the Science and Technology Backyard (STB) of China Agricultural University. As a group of 26 students, we mark the first batch of African students to participate in the program as China Agricultural University embarks on a mission to transform agriculture at the lowest level of smallholder farmers from China all the way to Africa. An introduction to the STB program had already been made theoretically during our first six months at China Agricultural University.

Initial impressions started before arriving at the research station in Quzhou as along the way we were able to witness farm activities that included grape farms, wheat, peach, sunflower, just to mention a few. Looking at all this brings hope that if we utilize this precious time and opportunity that we have here in China, we African students can harness a great deal of knowledge and technology in agriculture which we can bring back home to Africa and help to transform our continent in matters regarding food security, nutrition and empowering smallholder farmers who make the majority of stakeholders of agriculture in Africa. To achieve that, we need to pay utmost attention to the process that Chinese farmers especially smallholder farmers which STB program is currently working to address issues concerning this important aspect of agriculture. To reiterate the importance of STB in Africa I will briefly express the situation of agriculture in my country Tanzania. Agriculture is the main part of Tanzania's economy. As of 2016, Tanzania had over 44 million hectares of arable land with only 33 percent of this amount in cultivation. Almost 70 percent of the poor population live in rural areas, and almost all of them are involved in the farming sector. Land is a vital asset in ensuring food security, and the nine main food crops in Tanzania are maize, sorghum, millet, rice, wheat, beans, cassava, potatoes, and bananas. In order to have a successful STB program in Tanzania, all stakeholders in the agriculture industry must be linked together to facilitate transfer of knowledge and technology but also to make it easier for research projects to have impact on smallholder farmers.

This is where we as pioneers of this program come in. With lessons learned from China, agriculture in Africa can be transformed for the better. Coming back to our trip to Quzhou, we arrived at the station at around 3:30 pm on 2nd June, 2020. First impressions involved the presence of efficient facilities for learning including farm machinery, glasshouses, modern irrigation systems and equipment, desirable housing facilities for staff and students equipped with all the required necessities like water, electricity and internet. With all these available, as students felt duty to fulfill our mission to learn from the research station by integrating smoothly with the local smallholder farmers with the help from administrators, academic supervisors and Chinese students of China Agricultural University who were at the station for their various research projects. It was my hope that, as days go by, we will fulfill our goal of learning the best ways to cooperate with smallholder farmers in order to find solutions to various challenges in the process of crop production, which will ultimately impact agriculture in Africa as we will take this new knowledge and experience back home and use it to benefit our societies. Lastly, I would like to appreciate the warm welcome, assistance and cooperation from STB administrators.

Orientation and working environment at Quzhou Experimental Station

June 3rd, 2020 marked our second day at Quzhou research station in Hebei province as we arrived on the day before. We started the day at 8:30 am with going around the station for orientation under the supervision of Professor Jiao. The orientation aimed at making us familiar with the working environment of the experimental station. The main highlights of the orientation involved field trial areas, experimental fields, machinery and equipment.

At field trial areas we were able to see and briefly study on the ongoing research experiments on wheat, sunflowers and cowpeas. With wheat trials we were able to see how different fertilizer application treatments had effect on the growth and yield performance of wheat. The treatments involved different levels on nitrate and phosphate fertilizers or absence of either one of nitrate or phosphate fertilizer. For example, at one wheat field trial, absence of phosphate fertilizer resulted in delayed growth which eventually led to presence of green straws even though it was time already for harvesting as it was visible to the field trial that was supplied with both phosphate and nitrate fertilizer. The experiments also highlighted that the differences in fertilizer application among different blocks can be shown by the length of ear, size of grains and the yield obtained after harvest.

From this experimental area we went on to look at the equipment and machinery inventory available at Quzhou Experimental Station. We were able to learn about modern combine harvesters for wheat, maize and soybean. Also, planters, power tillers and ploughs. It was refreshing to get the idea of how these modern machines performs different farm activities with high level efficiency and performance which saves time for the farmer.

Study tour on irrigation water use and management in Quzhou

On June 10, 2020, we visited smallholder farms around Quzhou under the supervision of Professor Hongyan Zhang in an effort to understand and learn water use and management for irrigation for smallholder farmers in Quzhou. Our study started early in the morning at around 9:00 am. We took two mini vans as transport means. Our study tour aimed to understand two models of irrigation that were currently used by smallholder farmers in Quzhou. First is for smallholder farmers who are located either along the river banks or those within the vicinity of the river who can be reached easily by constructed water channels from the river. Second are those smallholder farmers situated far away from the river such that they cannot benefit directly from using the river water for irrigation. Therefore, in the first case of smallholder farmers close to the river, small water pumps are used to move water from the river to the field. This is not only a convenient approach but also relatively cheaper as farmers only pay for electricity, in this case gas for generator pumps.

For our first visit of the day, we started with a group of smallholder farmers near a channel of irrigation water. They employ a method where they pump water from the stream to the field. Professor Zhang explained to us that these farmers only incur the cost involved in pumping water from the irrigation channel which for this group of farmers is around 5 Yuan per mu. Our second visit was also another group of farmers close to the river channel but they are being provided irrigation water by the village irrigation water manager who supervises water distribution and oversees the supply unit with electrified pump. On this approach the cost for farmers is slightly higher as farmers pay around 20 Yuan per mu. However, in this approach farmers can put their own irrigation infrastructure from the river channel if they desire so which can bring down the cost to around 5 Yuan per mu. From here, we went on to visit a water distribution and management center for irrigation in Quzhou where among other things we learnt how water for irrigation is channeled from the main river to the irrigation channels and also, we learned about flood control system at the site where they utilize a basin structure which acts as a reservoir during periods of excess water to help to control flooding. After this visit we went to visit farmers who are far away from the river irrigation systems where for their case they use either shallow or deep wells for irrigation. Most of these farmers grow wheat and maize and compared to farmers that are close to the river, farmers that use water wells for irrigation incur more cost for irrigation as it is more expensive to pump water from underground. However, a lot can be done when it comes to water management as from our visit, we noticed flood irrigation is still prominent for most farmers which is not economical when irrigation water optimization is concerned. All in all, our visit was very educational and a lot of aspects of the irrigation system in Quzhou can be adopted in Africa and help move agriculture and food security as a whole to greater heights.

An epic visit to Xianggongzhuang STB and Zhangzhuang STB and a Primary Schools

June 4th, 2020, wasn't a typical day for a group of nine students including me who had the pleasure and honor of visiting STB sites in the nearby village. A short trip started at around 7:40 am from Quzhou Experimental Station to the village with the aim of understanding the inner workings of STB and connecting with the local community especially the future generation of farmers and also getting to know well the Chinese culture which brings even more benefits to us as it makes it easier for us to interact with local people and get to learn more. Now, our visit started by going to Xianggongzhuang STB where also we met students at Xianggongzhuang primary school. First and foremost, I must appreciate the warm welcome that we received from the school administration, which was quite impressive and refreshing for us. Another thing that impressed us was the fact that this was an STB site integrated with young students who grow up learning and appreciate farming and not just casual farming but modern agriculture that follows good agricultural practices and principles of sustainable farming. At this school we had the honor to present the kids with sport equipment like basketballs, table tennis and paddles, footballs and other sport supplies. Not only did we do that but also we had some quality time playing together with the students as a gesture of friendship and cooperation between China and Africa. The experience at Xianggongzhuang primary school has a profound significance in understanding the Chinese culture and tradition that are also important in understanding the economic activities of an area such as agriculture for our case. Also, it cements the existing interaction and cooperation. I must also express my sincere gratitude to the Xianggongzhuang primary school administration and to the young students for having us and showing us the other side of Chinese society—it was a real pleasure.

The next stop was yet another STB primary school. Like the previous STB, here also we were warmly welcomed by the head of school and other staff that were available. Our tour of the compound started with a heroic story of brave men and women from that area that participated in resolving the tragic calamity of corona virus that was recently put China on a rough and hard path. The head of school showed us pictures of nurses and doctors from around this area who stood at the front line during the crisis to help the country get back to normal and save lives. He also explained the reason they had a display of these brave men and women was to show an example to the students of how members of society must stand for one another all the time and even more so during tough times like the corona virus crisis where due to the togetherness of people and willingness to help each other the damage was greatly reduced and the virus of almost defeated as of now. We concluded the visit by going around the school campus where it was refreshing to see the beautiful orchards of grapes, apple, peach and persimmon.

Field tour of Wangzhuang STB for demonstration of wheat harvest

On June 6, 2020 we made an important study tour of Wangzhuang STB for the purpose of demonstration of wheat harvesting. The study tour started at around 8:00 am to Wangzhuang STB which is only a few miles from Quzhou Experimental Station as it took us not more than 10 minutes to arrive. A brief introduction of Wangzhuang STB was given by Professor Jiang Rongfeng who also went on to explain to the students about the overall process of wheat production from planting to harvesting.

Professor Rongfeng explained to us that Wangzhuang STB is a cooperation of the CAU with smallholder farmers of Quzhou who work together to realize the best, sustainable and cost-effective ways of producing wheat and maize. He explained for example the wheat crop that was present at the moment was a high yield variety that was being produced by using modern farming methods that consider proper spacing, mechanization (use of tractors for planting and harvesting), and other integrated systems such as the use of GPS in planting to ensure proper row planting and spacing. The existing variety which was ready for harvest is a high yield variety as it can produce a minimum of 9 tons of yield per hectare or more. He also explained that the STB is operated in such a way to empower smallholder farmers with this technology so that later on they will be able to utilize these techniques by themselves therefore achieving the goal of STB which is to promote technology and knowledge transfer for smallholder farmers which will result in more efficient and sustainable agriculture characterized by high yield and profits.

Professor Rongfeng Jiang also emphasized on the importance of careful observation of planting and harvesting season and it is a vital aspect in ensuring efficiency in production. For instance, in the case of Wangzhuang STB, when wheat crop is ready for harvesting, there shouldn't be any delays as it will affect the cycle of next crop which is maize in this case. After a period of information and details about the production process of wheat crop, it came to the moment we were all looking forward to—the harvesting of wheat using a combine harvester machine. As the machine started harvesting it was clear and open that it is important for traditional farming to graduate to utilize mechanization in farming as the machine was able to harvest a significant portion of the field within a short period of time. It not only saves time but also reduces the strain of labour involved in the process of harvesting and separating individual wheat grains from ears of wheat crop and thus increasing efficiency in production. After the wheat harvesting demonstration, we went on to observe another important process of measuring the moisture content of wheat grains. This process is important as it ensures the right dryness of the grains before they undergo further processing. Without doing so, the quality of the wheat can not be compromised as the grains are required to be in the right amount of moisture content. After having witnessed all these processes we thanked all the staff of CAU STB including Professor Rongfeng Jiang and Professor Xiaoqiang Jiao, and we took some photos together as memories of that important event.

The proposal defense of Sino-African STB masters students

June 26, 2020 was the last of two days for proposal defense of Sino-African

STB masters students. First, I should use this opportunity to appreciate effort and dedication shown by our CAU professors who formed the committee for vetting and providing suggestions for each and every one of us students. A total of 34 students presented proposals for their research starting from yesterday June 25, 2020. As for me, my presentation was today where I defended my proposal on the challenges facing extension agents in knowledge and technology transfer in rural Tanzania. After my presentation I got very instructive and constructive remarks from professors in the panel. One of the interesting suggestions I got is to utilize my time in Quzhou to learn about the develop approaches of rural China. Overall, the session gave us suggestions and ideas that would help us to improve our research and general understanding of research work which would make us more competent in the academic field. This will ultimately help us in the future as we are expected to be the frontiers of change in the agricultural sector in our respective countries.

Reflecting on my research topic: Extension Services in Tanzania

The majority of Tanzanian farmers are small-scale farmers who depend mainly on agriculture for their livelihoods. Agriculture provides food for their families and cash to meet their daily needs such as housing and school fees. To meet the family food and financial demands, small-scale farmers are obliged to adhere to good agricultural practices which are fundamental for high productivity. Economically feasible and socially acceptable management practices are needed to counter challenges of pests and diseases as well as to improve farming practices. Agricultural extension is essential for providing spaces for experimentation and innovation where new technologies can be explored.

Tanzania has been putting much emphasis on modernization of agriculture, and agricultural extension has been (as is today) seen as a means for achieving this objective. Heavy investments have been made in the agricultural sector because of the fact that the majority of Tanzanians live in rural areas and rely on agriculture for their employment and livelihood. Agricultural extension in Tanzania has been and still remains almost entirely financed by the public sector. Over time the focus of extension has been on transfer of technology that made the government to adopt systems and/or approaches to extension that have been mere extrapolation of approaches in donor countries and have essentially been supply driven, top-down approaches. The adopted systems/approaches never took into consideration farmers' issues, problems, needs and their involvement. In addition, they never undertook systematic investigation of what farmers expect from extension and of the role it should play. As a consequence, they ended up promoting and disseminating recommendations that were incompatible to local circumstances.

The agricultural extension system in Tanzania has faced many problems, of which the key seems to be the poor institutional, administrative and organizational structure of the extension services. Recently, the Tanzanian government, with the assistance of the World Bank, launched a major restructuring of the country's extension system including the introduction of the training and visit (T and V) extension. The T and V extension has some inherent weaknesses particularly if implemented without any modification to the Tanzanian context, due to lack of resources and other complimentary services. Recommendations are given to make the T and V system of extension more effective under Tanzanian conditions. The current organization of the extension system limits farmer accessibility to extension services in several ways: First of all, because of the dispersed nature of the field staff, few farmers have direct contact with these agents when necessary. One extension field worker is on average responsible for about 2 villages or 100 farm families, which means that the extension worker cannot be realistically expected to work with all the farmers under his/her jurisdiction. This problem is compounded by the poor working conditions of the field staff where by and large, means of travel are not available, while funds to pay for travel expenses are virtually non-existent. Through my research, I intend to survey the current situation of extension services in rural parts of Tanzania so as to understand the challenges of extension agents in Tanzania.

Return to Beijing and what lies next

Our stay in Quzhou was very important in the overall practical knowledge and skills development since we were able to actively participate in various activities which included research tests, excursions and field tours, workshops and presentations. Now we are back at west campus of China Agricultural University. During this time, we continue to work on analyzing data collected in our research tests in Quzhou. Also, during this time, we have to communicate closely with supervisors for advice on how to proceed well with the remaining part of our academic research. There is still a lot of work to be done but with the cooperation we are getting from the CAU STB staff, we expect all to go well until the final day of our study in China. At the moment as we continue with this academic process, we can't help but enjoy this winter moment and hope for the best as we approach the end of 2020 and welcome 2021 which is around the corner. I would like to conclude by expressing my sincere gratitude and appreciation to the CAU team who have put a lot of effort and dedication in ensuring us a smooth stay and study environment for us. Happy new year to everyone in advance!

The summary of my history at China Agricultural University and Quzhou Experimental Station

Wakjira Gurmesa Djano

The first-semester class started

I took a total of nine courses in the first semester: eight on the west campus of China Agricultural University and one at the east campus, which was elementary Chinese. After that our college planed for us to learn the practical one for six months at Quzhou Experimental Station, Quzhou county, Hebei province. As we finished the first semester, COVID-19 occurred. I was frustrated because our program was disturbed for a time being and I couldn't go out from the campus and every traffic stopped until June. After that I discussed with Professor Jiang Rongfeng about research title and selected the title of my research proposal "Effect of combined application of organic and inorganic fertilizer on the growth, yield and yield components of maize" and he approved it. I started to write my proposal research and side by side did meta-analyses on the effect of combined application organic resources and nitrogen fertilizer on maize yield. Until June, I have collected fifty-four research articles.

Journey from China Agricultural University (CAU) to Quzhou Experimental Station

On June 02, 2020, I started my journey from China Agricultural University

(CAU), Beijing at the time 9:20 am and arrived at Quzhou Experimental Station at the time of 3:15 pm. The objectives of going Quzhou Experimental Station are to learn the technology and to conduct field research.

The reception was very good and they took us to the dorm and gave us the key to our dorm. The reason I went to Quzhou was to do practical research and to visit different science and technology backyards (STBs). I stayed in Quzhou Experimental Station for six months (June 2, 2020 to November 22, 2020). During this time I did many work related to my education especially the field experiment and different field visits. When I started working with the people of Quzhou County, Hebei, they were very sociable with us and they looked us as their children. They motivated me to do my work with them, and especially I would like to thank the community of Quzhou Experimental Station for everything. I did my field experiment in Quzhou Experimental Station on the effect of combined application of cattle manure and inorganic fertilizer on growth, yield, and yield components of maize. In six months of my field experiment I did a good thing with supervisor Professor Jiang Rongfeng and Professor Yang. I learned many things from them and I would like to thank both professors.

I visited many factories in Quzhou. As I mentioned in the above, the people of Quzhou is wise people because they think all things positively. They treated all the students the same way, no matter we were from China or from other countries.

I have got many things from them socially and culturally. The Chinese people believed in the equality of human being whether you are male or female, black or white, rich or poor. Because of these, I appreciate the Chinese government and the Chinese people who developed this behavior in their generation. When I was in Quzhou we visited many areas of agriculture, such as: Mushroom factory A chicken farm Apple farm Factory of Organic fertilizer, Grape farm and Different farmer's fields.

At Quzhou Experimental Station I got a lot of experience. It was winter and the North China Plain was known for producing winter wheat. There were different activities on the field, especially how they used different fertilizers such as phosphorous, nitrogen, and mixed ones. I identified a field that has no phosphorous and its impacts on the maturity, production, and productivity of wheat. And also I have seen the field which has no nitrogen and its impacts on the production and productivity of wheat. The field which used both P and N was more productive in the Quzhou Experimental Station. I got experience to see the agricultural machines. There were a lot of machines in this station, big and small, for ploughing, fertilizer application, sowing, and harvesting. The last one I visited was the pots experiment place where the Chinese students were doing pots experiment in the greenhouse.

From the mushroom factory: I got a lot of things, such as how the mushroom was growing, what were the materials used for mushroom and how it was managed. This is the first time for me to see the factory of mushroom as it is not known in our country.

I have got good opportunities to visit these mushroom factories and I even tasted the mushroom—it is delicious. From that day I started to eat mushroom as a common food and now it is my stable food.

Chicken farm: The second of the field visit was the chicken farm. The owner of that chicken farm had 5,400 layers of chicken and he got 5,000 eggs per day and he managed his farm excellently. He was not only producing eggs but also producing manure for farmers.

Apple farm: The third one was the apple farm. As they introduced, the farmers had used that land for the cereal crops, but after the China Agricultural University established the Science and Technology Backyard (STB), the professors and students changed the mind of the farmers who started to plant apple and the farmers were benefiting from the apple farm rather than the previous one. I visited the apple farm with two Science and Technology Backyard (STB) Chinese students to learn how to manage the apple farm and I took two soil sample tests. I got good knowledge from these students and the owner of the apple farm and the community around there.

Factory of organic fertilizer: When I was going to visit the factory of organic fertilizer from Science and Technology Backyard (STB) I woke up at 6:00 am and the bus was in front of the international building and I didn't eat my breakfast and I went without breakfast because I was latecomer that day. I have got a lot of experience from them how they calculated the balance of each and everything they used. China is the first one in the world to consume chemical fertilizer and that factory is doing organic fertilizer to reduce the consumption of chemicals fertilizer. And they are doing it in a good manner and the ingredients are from cattle manure, chicken manure, swine manure, and goat and sheep manure. I learnt good knowledge from this organic factory.

Grape farm: I have seen the grape farm from one Science and Technology

Backyard (STB). Most of the Chinese students were doing their research on the grape but it was new for me. I even tasted grape after I came to China. There are many technologies in China that I can copy in my country. I missed this day because I exchanged many experiences with the Chinese farmers and the officials of Agriculture of Quzhou county governments and Chinese students, especially who were conducting their research on the grape.

Learned from farmers

I took one course after I came to Quzhou Experimental Station by a Professor Zhang on Advances in Resource Utilization and Plant Protection Technology. From this professor, I learned many things because he thought us many things related to this course. Even I learned different social life from him and he was an excellent teacher and I haven't seen such a teacher in my life education. Most of the North plain of China farmers use irrigation because there is low precipitation and it is not enough for crops. Most of the farmers use drip and furrow irrigation and sometimes there is sprinkle irrigation on a big farm and their life is not dependent on the rain only. Because of this, they harvest twice per year high quality and quantity crops from their field and they use modernized technology. In addition, the ministry of Quzhou county agriculture supports in all directions and when the farmers sow the seed and harvest the grain they are with the farmers. There is good cooperation between the farmers, Quzhou Experimental Station, and the ministry of agriculture in Quzhou county and farmers come to Quzhou Experimental Station and I learned even from the Chinese farmers.

Sharing experiences with elementary Chinese students

There was one elementary school around the Quzhou Experimental Station and I went there to teach them several times and they visited us one day in Quzhou Experimental Station. We had a good time with those students and their teachers and the government of Quzhou county and also with our professors.

Different farmers' field: I visited different farmers' fields, especially at the harvesting time of wheat and maize. When we visited the field of farmers, the Chinese farmers were very happy with us and they loved African students and they gave us what they had because of their love, I wanted to go and visit them every day if I got a chance. The farmers of Quzhou county used agricultural machines for harvesting wheat and maize and to sow the crops and for harvesting their grain. Even some times when I went out I practiced driving the machines which they used for sowing and harvesting. I got a good chance to visit the farmers' field and experienced technology the Chinese farmers used.

My story in China and Quzhou Experimental Station

Ibrahim Aliyu Usman

My journey to Quzhou Experimental Station from Beijing

We left Beijing on the 2nd of June, 2020, to Quzhou Experimental Station in Quzhou county, where we would carry out our field researches and acquaintance with agriculture in Chinese aspect. We were provided with safety things like face masks, alcohol sprays for use along the way, and during our initial stay at the experimental station. It was an exuberant and audacious one. As we drove out of Beijing getting near to the countryside of Beijing, it was not too much difference in aspect of the road network. It was a smooth road with bold signs on it. Good-looking mountains and structures could be seen from a distance along the way and activities like outstanding and advanced farming systems could be viewed through the fast-moving bus. We were welcomed warmly by the station staff and other students when we arrived at Quzhou Experimental Station. We were assigned our accommodations which had extremely encouraging studying and decent living amenities.

Field experiment in Quzhou Experimental Station

Soil sample was first collected in the experimental field of the research. The soil sample was collected using soil auger and a rubber hammer and it was collected using the S shape method of soil collection. The soil was collected at ten different locations in the experiment field at the depth of 20cm each hole. After the sample has been collected it was packed in a nylon bag and taken to the open greenhouse for sun drying. It took about three days before the soil was properly dried. The dried soil sample was then smashed into smaller particles using a wooden roller and sieved using a sieve and put into a bag. It was finally taken to the laboratory for final analysis.

Land clearing was the next agenda after collecting the soil samples. There were few plants, grasses and weed in the field that needed to be cleared from the farm. Ploughing machine attached to a tractor was used to clear all the unwanted plants in the field. After the land clearing, the field was also tilled using same tractor to soften the soil for easy emergence of the crops after planting. Planting was the next step after the clearing of the land. Maize cultivar Denghai 605 was planted in the field at a row spacing of 60cm and plant spacing of 20cm and at a depth of 10cm Two maize seeds were planted per hole. Three days after planting, the field was watered using pipe irrigation because the soil was becoming dried. A week after planting all the planted seeds emerged and it was the right time to apply fertilizer. Demarcation of the field was also done by local farmers to differentiate between various treatments and replication. Each plot of the treatment is 6m by 3m for all treatments.

My experiment was on phosphorus fertilizer application on maize. In the laboratory prior to the fertilizer application day, I measured all the amount and types of fertilizer to be applied on the experimental field according to the treatments and replications I had for the research. A week after planting, fertilizer was applied using a local tool for the application at the depth of 10cm. Among the fertilizers I used were ammonium polyphosphate (APP), diammonium phosphate (DAP), urea and potassium chloride (KCL).

After a month of planting, it happened that some insects were eating some parts of the plants. Insecticide was diluted in a knapsack sprayer and was used to fumigate all the experimental field and its surroundings. There was no data to collect at this stage so the crops were growing well.

The first data collection was at tasseling stage, where there were so many parameters to take which included SPAD reading, leaf length, plant height, leaf width, fresh and dry biomass, leaf area index and nutrient content. SPAD reading is the measurement of chlorophyll content in a particular plant. This was done using the SPAD meter placing the meter on the leaf that was directly under cob of the maize plant. It was measured three times and the average was recorded. Three plants were harvested from each of the twenty plots of the experiment. Each plant was measured and recorded, measurement including plant height, leaf height, leaf width, and total number of leaves in each plant. After that, the leaves were separated from the stem and all were chopped into smaller pieces for easy and quick drying. Weight of the fresh biomass was also recorded before sun drying. It took more than ten days before the samples dried due to low temperature of the environment. The samples were also taken to the lab for oven drying. We dried the sample for three days in the oven and when it was properly done, dried weight of the biomass was also recorded and the samples were given to local farmers for grinding before the nutrient analysis.

The final stage was the harvest. Unlike the previous data collected, this was entirely different. Here the parameters were yield and yield component, fresh and dry biomass, nutrient content and soil sampling. Prior to the harvest a tutorial was given to us on how to get all these data accordingly. We were at the experimental field and it was shown to us practically. We got all the necessary things for the harvest like net bag, scissors, measuring tape, knife, weighing scale etc. For yield, since each plot is 6m × 3m divided into exactly two i.e., 3m × 3m, all the maize cobs in the other half were removed from the plants and put to one net bag according to the treatments. Another three plants were uprooted from the other half of the plots which would be used to analyze nutrient content at the harvest stage. The cobs for yield and yield components are measured at fresh stage and recorded then you select five uniform maize cobs among them that will be used for oven drying.

Those five cobs were also measured: their total weight, diameter of each cob and total number of kernels on each cob.

Three other plants that were uprooted in the other half of the field were also measured: plant height, cob height, ear height, cob diameter and fresh biomass respectively. Both the stem and the leaves were chopped into smaller sizes for easy and quick drying. Due to the weather presently, there was no sun to dry those samples so oven drying was used. Since all the samples were so fresh, it took a longer time in the oven to dry. It took almost a week for all the samples to get dried in the oven. After removing the samples from the oven, weight of the dry samples of the five cobs and other samples for the other parameters was measured. After removing them from the oven, the kernels were separated from the cobs and counted 500 grains three times and recorded the average of the kernels counted.

The dried stem, leaves and cobs were also measured and kernels were seperated from the cobs. This one was used for nutrient analysis. The dried biomass was smashed by the local farmers and taken to the laboratory for the final analysis.

The last stage of the experiment was the collecting of another soil sample, but this time the soil would be collected in every plot of the experiment because of the different types of fertilizer that were applied unlike the first soil sample that was collected. In each of the 20 plots I had, soil auger and a rubber hammer were used to extract the soil. In each plot, there were five rows and the soil sample was taken from the three middle rows of each plot and from each of the three rows of the middle rows. The samples were taken at 0-20cm and 20-40cm respectively. All of 0-20cm of a particular plot was put together in the same bag while samples collected at 20-40cm were also put together in the same bag. After collecting all the soil samples, we took them to the greenhouse for sun drying. The samples were dried separately and after 4-5 days of drying, a wooden roller was used to smash the dried soil samples into smaller particles and sieved with a sieve to remove unwanted particles that will temper the final analysis of the soil. All data for all the parameters were recorded in an Excel file and analyzed accordingly.

Excursions and field trips

Wangzhuang STB field visit

Wangzhuang STB was the first STB we visited in Wangzhuang village. On Saturday the 6th of June, 2020, the field was under the supervision of the Quzhou Experimental Station. At the field, there were already some STB students, farmers, and teachers who were waiting for us (African STB students) to arrive. It began with a brief introduction by Prof. Jiang Rongfeng informing us on all about the wheat farm. The combine harvester was in the position to give the audience a demonstration but before the demonstration took place, 4cm × 10cm row spacing was used in planting the wheat which was 10cm apart and the other 30cm space was left blank to plant maize after winter harvest. Innovative machineries were used from the beginning to the end of the cultivation. The combine harvester then started the demonstration of the harvesting procedure. Demonstration was given to us by Prof. Cui Zhenling about the whole technology behind the entire process.

Advances in resource utilization and plant protection technologies lecture

This was the first lecture that was given to us by Prof. Hongyan Zhang on the June 8, 2020. The title of the course was Advances in Resource Utilization and Plant Protection Technologies. The course was about how scholars innovated more help in advance knowhows of agriculture and to tackle major challenges of farming activities in China. However, he also discussed on how this advanced technology has made agricultural production so easy and efficient, which reduced cost of labor and time, meanwhile increased the production in all aspects of agriculture.

Visit to mushroom farm in Qiuxian

Prof. Zheng Suyue, a visiting lecturer from Hebei University of Engineering came to give us about mushroom production before proceeding to the farm where the production was taking place. The lecture took about an hour which was delivered in Chinese and being translated to English by Prof. Zhang. We then proceeded to where the mushroom was being cultivated. At the farm, soil, biochar, cow dung and husk are mixed to produce substrates for the production. The substrates can produce up to five different badges of the mushroom which is later used by farmers as fertilizer in the farmland. Temperature is well regulated in the mushroom production to ensure high yield.

Water resource management in Quzhou

A trip was organized by Prof. Zhang on 20th June, 2020 to go within the Quzhou county and discover how farmers use irrigation skills to manage the water in the community. Fuyang River is the major source of all the water in the community. It was linked through some artificial tunnels in which the farmers tapped from them with the use of water pumps to irrigate their farmlands. Most of these farmlands are located near the tunnels which they use pipes to irrigate the plants. Some of the farmers whose farmlands are far from the tunnels construct wells within the farmyard and connect them to electricity and source water for irrigation but it is more expensive. In some other part of the county, some farmers builds deeper well compared to the others.

After touring most of the tunnels and rivers across the county, we finally stopped at an STB station which was managed by some CAU students. That demonstrated to us the relevance and importance of drip irrigation and how it solved water problem in the region.

My unforgettable life in Beijing, China

Aminu Hussaini Adamu

From blindness to sight

Upon arrival at the Chinese airport, things were different from what I thought. I had definitions and assumptions of China in my mind, a lot of basic assumptions and expectations of how China should look like and to my surprise all the assumptions and expectations were superseded by the realities at my sight. Coming from the most populous country in Africa—Nigeria, China population is the first in the world but to my judgment is the most secured and controlled population on the earth. Thanks to my host and efficient technology of communication and map of China I was able to get to my accommodation a day after my arrival. It was quite an experience, the journey and the destination. That day I met my fellow Nigerians Hamed who took me to international student building to an eatery for a dinner; it's not my first time outside the country but my first to Asia and China. That day I sat in a restaurant where the meal was prepared right on spot and in front of me and that time was my first experience of the Chinese dishes. I ate dumplings: the food was literally melting in my mouth with a taste I would never forget. Looking at the architecture of the country a day after my arrival, I made a promise to go around China, visit a lot of tourism and historic centers, and explore China history before I left. That day I had no option but to take a lot of pictures and save to my social media wall and share to my family and friends for them to enjoy the experience I was in.

School and beyond

I had a BSc degree after attending elementary and secondary school back in Nigeria, but the China Agricultural University (CAU) international school is another level—it's not unrelated but the school activities are more practical and easy catching. It used to be very difficult for me to face a group of people I didn't know—it was like an unknowable force coming to me while presenting on a stage. The class engagement was the best way to improve myself. I think Research Methodology should be taught to anybody not only in graduate class but also in any work premise for them to understand how one variable can directly or indirectly affect another and how factorial analysis can help you understand how different variables affects a given factor. It was actually my favorite class. The Chinese history class also interested me because I ended up learning a lot from it.

The class group gave me that big victory feeling to just be part of the nice people from different parts of the world. We were learning a lot from each other. Each one of us came from different countries and walks of life. Some outside class discussions were sometimes much more interesting than the class ones, to share our insights about the political views, religious and socioeconomic understanding. My roommates were much more interesting: Abdullahi, Aliyu, Lawal and Erons were fun to be around. We sometimes cooked and ate out and visited some places together. It was difficult to get away from the family and friends but these people filled up the space in my life.

Edge of the world (The Great Wall of China)

One of the wonders of the world ever exist is the Great Wall of China in north of China, of over 20,000 km and an average of 8 meters high built to protect the northern China. The Great Wall was the oldest piece that I had come across my entire life. An excitement that I cannot keep to myself: that day I took more than two hundreds pictures and videos of which I shared more than fifty percent to make sure all my family and friends get a share of the experience. The experience that day kept me up late that night, as if I suddenly became an engineer, architect, economist and most importantly historian. It kept coming to my thoughts: how many people built this wall and how they got the materials to construct the wall. I missed the place even before I left it. I wanted to go back immediately after we left.

My journey from Beijing to Quzhou Experimental Station, Hebei province

I am one of the thirty four students of Science and Technology Backyard (STB) program. We left Beijing on 02.06.2020 early in the morning. All the 34 African students moved from CAU to Quzhou Experimental Station in Quzhou county, Hebei province where we would carry out our academic field experiments as well as get exposure to China's agricultural side. Before we left China Agricultural University, we were provided with safety materials like face masks, alcohol sprays for use along the way, and during our initial stay at the experimental station. The journey was a blissful and exploratory expedition as we moved from a cosmopolitan city to rural China. When we arrived at Quzhou Experimental Station, we were warmly welcomed by the experimental station staff and other students. We were allocated to our rooms which had excellent conducive studying and decent living facilities. After some hours, some of the Chinese students led us to the launch of a new farmer field school around Quzhou county. They were led by two professors from Quzhou Experimental Station, Prof. Jiang Rongfeng and Prof. Zhang Hongyan. After that the Quzhou Experimental Station management organized a meeting in the International Cooperation Centre building where we received an official welcome from all the station officials. Rules and regulations were shared with us such as regulations of dormitory, administration, restaurant management, regulations on the administration of safety-study room, provision on laboratory administration and other matters.

Dream hunter: My successful agricultural experiences in China

Food security is one of the most worrying issues of all states around the world and more specifically in this time of COVID-19 pandemic. According to FAO in 2019, in total 2 billion people (26.4%) of the world population are touched by food insecurity. The main victims of the hunger are rural area people. This situation is more alarmed in Africa with an increase in undernourishment almost everywhere. In 2017, more than 257 million people or 20% of Africa's population are suffering from hunger or lack of adequate dietary energy. About 59 million and 5% of children under five are stranded and overweight respectively (FAO, 2018). For example in my country Burkina Faso, more than 3.3 million people are facing acute food insecurity (FAO and WFP, 2020). Climate change, poverty, conflict, national policies, environmental degradation, trade barriers, inadequate agricultural development, population growth, low level of education, social and gender inequalities, unsanitary conditions, cultural insensitivity and natural disasters can be cited as the causes of the food insecurity in the world and particularly in Africa.

Despite its huge population (20% of world population) and natural resources limitation (only 9% of world farming land and 5% of world water resources), China in just two to three decades has been able to reduce even boosted hunger outside its borders. This is through the intensification of agricultural production, the development and use of technology and innovation in agriculture, the implementation of new approaches to the extension of agricultural technologies and the adoption and enforcement of policies in favour of this sector. Indeed, the main cereals like maize and wheat have seen the yield increased (from 2.09t/ha in 1970 to 6.32t/ha in 2019 for maize and from 1.08t/ha in 1969 to 5.41t/ha in 2018 for wheat). Science and Technology Backyard (STB) is an integrated platform for technology innovation, knowledge transfer, training and agricultural transformation towards sustainable intensification which has been a huge success and has extended through all China and has contributed a lot to agricultural transformation. Unlike in Africa, the performances of both crops are remained quasi stagnate (1.51t/ha and 1.6t/ha in 1990 to 2.04t/ha and 2.86t/ha for maize and wheat respectively) despite its huge population growing (From 1960, Africa's population grew to about 640 million in 1990 to 1.3 billion in 2019, or 17% of the world's population) (FAOSTAT, 2019). How Africa can change this situation and leave food insecurity?

Learn from Chinese experience in terms of agricultural technology and innovation and adapt it to African condition will be a solution for African countries to achieve food security for their people. It is into this optic that the Belt and Road & South-South Cooperation Agricultural Education, Science and Technology Innovation League has been created in 2018 with a vision to strengthening cooperation between the South-South countries in the field of Agricultural Education, Science and Technology. Supported by the Chinese Government Scholarship-Silk Road Program and in accordance with the principle of "strategy centred, pinpoint implementation, resource integration, joint advancements, advantage exploration, mutual benefits, based on the present and looking towards the future", the League will provide degree programs in agriculture for the students from the overseas member institutions and cultivate them into advanced talents in agriculture. The Sino-STB (Science and Technology Backyard) program, which has recruited and is training for three years 34 African students from 8 countries for a master's degree in resources utilization and plant protection in CAU is the concrete and visible implementation of the benefit of this South-South cooperation. I'm Zigani Saturnin, from Burkina Faso one of the Sino-Africa STB project students and I'm going to share with you my experience in China.

My experience in Beijing

Leaving my country Burkina Faso on September 20th, 2019 and after almost two days of flight with of course a few hours' stopovers in some countries like Niger and Ethiopia, our plane landed at Beijing International Airport on September 22, at about 5:00 pm. When I got off the plane I was amazed by the immensity and beauty of the airport. Accompanying by my compatriot Yameogo Philippe, we had a hard time finding our way because it was our first time out of Africa and being among so many people who moved everywhere. After several attempts to find the exit without success, we had been guided by a security guard to the exit that led to the taxi station. I had about ten days to complete the administrative conditions (registration to the police, registration to the university and in the rooms, and so on) before the actual start of the courses in October 2019.

For a period of five months, these theoretical courses were taught by eminent CAU professors. It was mainly a matter of sharing with us the model of change of Chinese agriculture and more specifically about the Science and Technology Backyard (STB) approach. The following modules were covered: organic farming, elementary chinese, efficient use of agro production, nonpoint source pollution of agriculture, thesis writing, biometrics and experimental design, rural revitalization and innovation and research integrity and academic norms. For each module, the student should do a personal search and make a presentation on a topic proposed by the teacher. Also, in order to combine theory with practice, we had to participate in several study trips to sites such as agro-ecological farms, laboratory and greenhouses etc.

My life during the COVID-19 time

The restriction due to the lockdown of the COVID-19 pandemic impacted my living condition in China. It was really a period of general panic around the world that had already recorded thousands of cases and deaths. For many countries, it was therefore a total panic with the lack of medical consumables for the effective care of the sick. I was really worried about my parents and especially my little family. In this state of general shock, initiatives had to be developed. This is why I created and led a Wechat group called FASO SOLIDARITE COVID-19 for Burkinabe living in China for a fundraiser to help our dear party in this difficult time. Thus, we were able to collect a modest sum of 1, 324 RMB which was donated to the first head of our national representation in China for delivery to the management committee of COVID-19 in Burkina Faso. A congratulatory letter was sent to us by Burkina Faso's ambassador to China for this noble initiative. This platform has also served as a channel for raising awareness among our compatriots in the country about the symptoms and manifestations of the disease and the preventive measures to see compliance with barrier gestures and the promotion of solidarity during the containment period. However, during this time of confinement my brother Philippe and I had kept in touch and worked closely with our supervisors of CAU (Professor Zhang Junling and Zhang Hongyan) and of the country (Dr. ZHAO Qinglu, coordinator of the Mil Project in Burkina Faso led by CGCOC group) in order to define our research themes and start literature reviews. Also, at the invitation of the supervisors, Philippe and I had expanded and shared our two bibliographic journals in an article for publication entitled: Cropping systems and fertilization mode in millet production in West Africa.

My story in Quzhou

The pandemic situation has calmed with the reduction of the number of cases. So, the University arranged for internship at Quzhou Experimental Station in Hebei province of North China Plain for all the Sino-African STB students.The objectives of this internship were to allow students to discover the Chinese country environment and to put into practice the knowledge acquired during the 5 months of theoretical courses and to implement research topics (conduct of experimental plots and pots, surveys, and so on). On the other hand, it was to see and touch technological changes and innovations in agricultural approach and practices and more specifically the STB approach with its positive impacts on agricultural production and the improvement of household living conditions in Quzhou county.

Following this schedule we started our journey to Quzhou Experimental Station on June 2, 2020. It was a great moment for me because it was my first time to leave of Beijing and cross the whole city and contemplate the beautiful landscape of China with all its great diversity. After six hours of driving, we arrived finally at Quzhou county and I was surprised at the infrastructural development level of this place. In fact, this village is more developed in terms of infrastructure than some of my country regions.

My performance in Quzhou Experimental Station

During my six months staying in Quzhou, I have dedicated myself on millet management and production systems in China. In fact, millet is the second major cereal crop and staple food in my country (Burkina Faso) after sorghum. It represents 20% of the cereal production with the low average yield (853kg/ha) compared to China which records 2,537kg/ha in 2018 (FAOSTAT, 2019). My purpose is to learn new techniques, technologies and good agricultural practices in millet management and production useful in

China which can be adapted in Burkina Faso's condition in order to increase millet yield. Exactly, my research topic is: "Comparison of millet and soybean intercropping systems response on nitrogen use efficiency in China and Burkina Faso". With a general objective to compare the effect of associated crop systems (millet/soybean) to increase nitrogen use efficiency, and improve both soil quality and agricultural production in China and Burkina Faso, this study was conducted in two steps: field trial and pot experimentation.

The first three weeks of June was devoted to the finalization of the drafting of research proposal both Word and PowerPoints versions followed by defence. Thus, the intensive and close work with my supervisors allowed me to move brilliantly to the final defence session on June 25 and 26, 2020 under the approval of a committee of professors from China Agricultural University.

Plot experimental design and implementation

The validation of my research proposal paved the way for the implementation of our various experimental designs with the support of my supervisors, a technician and my Chinese friend (Miss Li RAN). So, the first step of my research which was plot experiment started on June 19th, 2020 including the following activities: soil sampling, soil preparation operations, plants sampling, millet and soybean harvesting and yield assessment.

The preliminary results of my plot experimentation illustrated the benefit of millet/soybean intercropping system on nitrogen use efficiency. Indeed, in both densities (2:1; 3:1) of intercropping system, the millet average yield is higher for plots without nitrogen (5.355t/ha; 6.624t/ha) than those with nitrogen application (5t/ha; 6.354t/ha). Also, there is no significant difference among millet average yield in monocropping system without nitrogen (6.9t/ha) and with nitrogen application (7.049t/ha). However, this yield is around eight times than my country millet yield. Furthermore, the soybean nodules number is higher in all the treatments without than those with nitrogen application. For example in intercopping (3:1) system, there are 31 and 21 as average nodules number of soybean without nitrogen and soybean with nitrogen treatment respectively.

The second phase of my research had started on August 5th 2020 by millet and soybean seeds pre-germination in the laboratory and their plantation two days later. Same crops (millet and soybean) were used in monocropping and intercropping systems like in plot experiment. However, I added Mungbean in this experiment in order to compare its effects of soybean one on millets growing parameters in intercropping system. Totally, forty four pots were used with nitrogen application (60kg of N) or no nitrogen (N0) as main factor. Phosphorus (45kg/ha) and potassium (30kg/ha) have been used like base in all the treatment. Indeed, soil from the field was sifted with a 2mm fine mesh sieve and then mixed with the fertilizer dose and put in the pots before sowing. Also, seeds have been pre-germinated into the laboratory after being treated in Hydrogen peroxide solution (H_2O_2) for 10 minutes. After planting, crops maintenance operations such as: watering, thinning, weeding and sanitary treatment, plants growing parameters measurement like in field were done. Thus, two months after planting day, plants were harvested and plant shoots were dried, mashed and given to the laboratory for analysing the nutrient content. Before harvesting, plant shoots comparatives photos were taken in order to highlight the morphological and physiological differences between treatments. The same thing has been done for the roots after harvesting. Finally, all the roots were weighted and scanned in the laboratory.

The preliminary results showed the millet plants in intercropping system with soybean had a higher content of chlorophyll (31.9 SPAD) than mono-cropping one (23.6 SPAD). The same trend has been observed with the millet dry biomass weight (30.4g against 26g for intercropping system and mono-cropping system respectively). It means that the millet/soybean intercropping system is more efficient in term of nitrogen use than mono-cropping system.

In summary, the implementation of these activities (plot and pot experiments) allowed me to improve my knowledge in plot management, soil preparation, and especially the morphology and the physiology of Chinese millet. I have also learned about soil sampling and yield assessment and the pots experimental activities allowed me to have a mastering about the soil treatment process from seed pre-germination, plants' growing parameters measurement to plants maintenance in pots.

Visits to STB

The main purpose of our staying in Quzhou Experimental Station was to see, touch and live the STB approach and its results in terms of benefits for agricultural innovation and production, but also in improving farmers' living conditions. In these STBs, a group of scientists, university professors, students, and farmers' leaders sit together to discuss the problems of agricultural production, provide a possible solution together and finally implement the suggested solution together for the benefits of farmers. I was really amazed during these different visits. So, several visits marked my stay in the research station. Indeed, as soon as we arrived, a first visit led by Prof. Jiao allowed us to discover the center as a whole ranging from different compartments, equipment to experimental fields. In addition, in the logic of allowing us to discover the results achieved in the STB, visits were organized in the nearby STB villages. Thus, we participated in guided tours of the mechanized wheat harvest in Wangzhuang STB, apple and grape STBs in Xianggongzhuang and Qianya villages respectively. These visits allowed me to see the real intensification of agriculture and its impact on agricultural production. From my own experience with some visits in STBs, I can summarize this intensification into the following points: adoption and sustainable use of agricultural inputs (the mechanization, fertilizer, seed, and water); improving infrastructure and financial markets (road, irrigation, e-commerce, etc.); and creating and applying local knowledge and good political will of the government.

My experience in agricultural mechanisation in Wangzhuang STB

On June 6th, 2020, I took part in the wheat mechanical harvesting demonstration in Wangzhuang Science and Technology Backyard (STB). This field demonstration was an occasion of discovery for me. Firstly, it was my first time to see physically large intensified wheat field at maturity stage and to touch this plant, because we don't produce wheat in my country. So, all wheat flour is imported from neighbouring and European countries. Indeed, a combine machine was used for this harvesting operation. This machine performs at the same time the operations of harvesting, threshing, winnowing, and packing wheat grains. The same type of harvesting machine has been used to harvest my plot experimental millet. I confess I was really impressed by this technology because it was my first time to see and participate in it. It helps to save time, reduce yield loss and give the high grain quality after harvesting. In just one hour of work, this machine makes about 5 people performing for 3 days of work. For example, for my experimental field with an area about 0.5ha, this machine took less than 30 minutes to finish it.

In addition, during the implementation of my millet plot experiments in June 2020 at Quzhou, I used a manual machine for fertilizer burying into the soil. Indeed, after plots preparation, I spreaded the amount of fertilizer according to each treatment in plots and used this small machine to bury and mix it easily with soil before sowing my crop.

My visit in grape STB in Qianya village and in the mushroom farm opened my mind on the good opportunities which I would like to implement in my country after going back. In fact the culture of both crops is not developed in my country and I think introducing and developing the production of these crops can be a source of crop diversification but especially for food security due to the high nutritional value and medicinal virtues of mushroom. '

Adoption and sustainable use of agricultural inputs

The management of soil fertility by adopting good agricultural practices such as: soil restoration by the total incorporation of crop residues after harvest, crop rotation and intercropping systems, irrigation water reduction by soil protection with plastics... have allowed agricultural soils to retain good physical-chemical and organic properties for good plant growth (apple, grape). Also, the work of researchers, students in close collaboration with farmers and agricultural inputs firms (fertilizers, seeds and agricultural machinery) like Science and Technology Backyard (STB) approach has enabled the implementation of fertilizer formulas adapting to the initial soil conditions and plant's needs. In addition, the development and extension of new efficient crop varieties that meet market needs have facilitated increased agricultural production in rural China. For example, with STB approach, researchers have developed maize and wheat varieties that can achieve performance of 12t/ha and 9t/ha respectively. From personal experience, conducting research activities in my experimental plot on Chinese millet production systems in association with soybeans has given me amazing results far beyond my expectations. Indeed, in the mono-cropping system, I obtained yields in the order of 7t/ha and 4.6t/ha respectively for millet and soybeans. These different yields are ten and three times higher than millet and soybeans in Africa. By the way, variety performance is an important factor in yield, but also parameters such as plant density and soil amendment are to be taken into account. For example, millet density in China ranges from 300,000 to 500,000 plants/ha compared to less than 60,000 plants/ha in some African countries.

Furthermore, the development of irrigation system allows farmers to carry out the agricultural activity all year round and make their investments profitable. For example, in Quzhou county, the common seasonal crops rotation is winter-wheat and summer-maize, which allows farmers to immediately sow wheat after the maize harvest on farm and have two harvests in the year. Also, the development of e-commerce through various platforms such as WeChats Pays, Taobao, Pinduoduo and so on makes it possible to bring consumers closer to producers for the flow of agricultural products in China.

Finally the Chinese government's good policy of subsidizing agricultural inputs for farmers plays important role in the adoption and promotion of new technologies.

Courses participation in Quzhou

During my stay in Quzhou, I also "took" courses on the following topics: advances in resource utilization and plant protection, initiation on meta-analysis and China panorama. The first course has been led by my supervisor Mr. Zhang Hongyan. This course has really opened my mind and changed my vision on agricultural resource utilization through Chinese example. In fact, facing many challenges in agricultural production (lack of water in Northern part, soil salinity, air pollution, etc), the Chinese government worked closely with scientists and all the population to make a big change. For example, to solve the water problem in the North part, Chinese people made channels (West line, Middle line and East line) in the mountain to transport water from South to North China, about 500 km. Thus, this water is used by farmers for their field irrigation and that makes a big change in their living conditions. Besides that, the huge denoted "Initiating National Soil Testing and Fertilizer Recommendation Project" implemented by Chinese government and scientists in 2005 following the overuse of chemical fertilizers (330kg N/ha) with its damages in environment (eutrophication, soil acidification, diseases...) has really impressed me. Indeed, this project which has touched 200 counties in 2005 and 600 counties in 2006 has made it possible to know the nutrient content of soils in entire China, the development of new fertilizer formulations according to areas and technologies (smart phones, rapid on-farm soil testing, crops sensors, machines ...) and this accompanied by field experiment, training publicity through the extension system and the STB allowed China to reduce in 10 years its consumption of fertilizers and increase crops yields. This course has been followed by an excursion which allowed me to see and touch the results of this project in Quzhou county.

Seminars and reportage participations

Many seminars about my or other classmates' literature review and/or meta-analysis progress served as occasions to learn from each other which helped me to improve my own work. Also, in the second week of June, as part of the preparations for the visit of the Director of CAU and the leaders of Hebei province, I developed and presented a poster on the topic "Millet production in Burkina Faso and adapted technologies in Quzhou". This poster was appreciated by teachers and served as an example for my colleagues. The review version of this poster has been presented during the visit of Chinese Ministry of Agriculture in early July and during the commemoration of the World Food Day.

Furthermore, for the visibility of STB activities, I have been a leading actor in several television reportages and online journals such as: (i) Foreign students take part in agricultural practice activities in Hebei; (ii) Competition of the best producer of grape in Qianya STB; (iii) Sharing experience with high school and middle school students as part of the commemoration of International Food Day; (iv) Reportage about my experience in Quzhou: Apprentissage des *cultures* in French version (currently under recording).

Paper writing and work capitalisation

In terms of paper writing, I was doing the meta-analysis on the topic: Effects of nitrogen fertilization response on millet yield in Africa. As of today, I have able to collect about forty articles with 390 observations that I entered into an Excel database. I will still continue data collection and hope to finish with this by the end of December 2020 in order to start the project analysis. This exercise allowed me to improve my method of document search (the use of search engines such as Web of Science, Google Scholar, Bing and so on) and my ability to read and critically analyze scientific works on the one hand but also to familiarize myself with data extraction and analysis software such as GetData, QGIS geo-software, etc. Besides that, I am a co-author of the article about the cropping system and fertilization mode of millet in West Africa which has been submitted to the journal for publishing.

In addition, one of the most important things was writing the daily reports of my activities. In effect, these reports allowed me to take stock of my activities on a daily basis, to list the difficulties encountered and to outline the prospects for solutions and the planning of the next day. This is an effective tool for monitoring our activities by our supervisors. From the 2nd June to the present days I have written two hundred and three working diaries. As a lesson learned, it allowed me to improve my ability to write, synthesize and capitalize data, but also to have a global view of my experiences in China and particular at the Quzhou Experimental Station.

Cultural integration

In terms of cultural integration, I participated in a cultural day organized by the farmers of wheat STB village on the occasion of the Mid-Autumn Day. Added to this was the night of cultural sharing between Chinese and African students organized at the resort. On this occasion I participated in the board games and proposed a documentary film on the cultural potential of my country Burkina Faso. In addition, with the aim to promote English in schools and motivate students to like and practice this language, I was chosen with some classmates to administer an English course in "Si Tuan" middle school nearby last mid-October 2020. Topics like greeting, human body parts, colours, names of fruits and foods, etc. were approached. The collective sports (gym, football, basketball) ended this visit to the great pleasure of the students and teachers.

Finally on a relational level, I maintained a very good relationship of communication, friendship and fraternity with my fellow Chinese students whom we really get on well and do sports (badminton and table tennis) and cultural activities together (participation in the party). As for the local people, I enjoyed working closely and communicating with farmers with a spirit of learning good agricultural practices but also into optic to improve my expression of the Chinese language.

Perspectives

One year in China has been really fruitful for me. It enabled me to have new experiences in the domain of agricultural technologies and innovation, resource utilization efficiency on the one hand, and experiment and the STB approach on the other hand. This forged in me a new person, who after going back in Africa hopes to establish STB model with the support of the government for the happiness especially of poor households. This will be through some key actions such as:

- Organize the STB seminars to my colleagues at the Ministry of Agriculture, responsible for agricultural universities and farmers leaders;
- Apply the STB approach with a few voluntary producers;
- Mentor students with the STB approach;
- Provide modules on the STB approach at my country's Agricultural Universities in collaboration with CAU;
- Initiate and develop a strong partnership between CAU and the agricultural universities of my country.

I would like to make a special mention and thank all the teachers for their unwavering support in conducting my research. I quote: Prof. Zhang Hongyan (my supervisor), Prof. Zhang Junling (co-supervisor), and Professor Jiang Rongfeng, Prof. Jiao Xiaoqiang, Prof. Zhang Chaochun and others. I give special thanks to CGCOC Group for sponsoring my studies in China.

Aminu 和他的中国朋友在植物园合影

Aminu 和中国学生完成试验布置后合影

Bilisuma 和 Saturnin 走在田间的小路上

Bilisuma 在温室打理盆栽试验

Bilisuma 和 Saturnin 测量玉米株高

Buana 和 David 顶着炎炎夏日取样

David 与王庄村的小孩合影

Eric 为曲周县第四疃镇当地小学生讲解试验

Odige 为盆栽试验浇水

OLa 和 Belay 在实验站完成试验后合影

Ola 与白寨科技小院学生在农户示范田

Philipe 和中国学生讨论试验布置

Phillpe 和张朝春教授在科技小院讨论农民赋能问题

Phillpe 在曲周实验站学习甜叶菊移栽技术

Priscila 和 David 在实验站讨论修改每月工作简报

Saturnin 在曲周实验站开展谷子密度田间试验

Saturnin 与中国学生一起做试验

Solomon 在果园进行果树套袋试验

Wakjira 向老师请教发现的玉米病害

白寨科技小院研究生为 Belay 和 Chagga 解答问题

劳动间隙，村民为 Saturnin 擦汗

迪诺向前衡科技小院的学生请教葡萄种植技术

迪诺在三百亩试验基地开展田间试验

David、Erick 等非洲留学生在王庄学习农机操作

江荣风教授给留学生讲授果园管理技术

江荣风教授为 Solomon 和 Wakjira 答疑解惑

留学生参观德众科技小院

留学生参观滏阳河水利设施

曲周县县委书记李凡同志关心留学生们
在曲周的生活

留学生参观相公庄苹果科技小院

留学生在岳庄参加农民田间学校活动

留学生在曲周育苗园区学习

留学生在前衙科技小院参加葡萄品鉴大赛

留学生在曲周实验站参加世界粮食日活动

留学生在前衙科技小院观察葡萄新品种

张宏彦和吕振宇老师带领留学生进行野外实践

留学生和村民一起工作

留学生在前衙科技小院开展支教活动

留学生和中国学生在前衙村合影

留学生接受曲周县电视台采访

2019级留学生顺利完成开题答辩

2019级留学生在曲周完成6个月的实践教育

留学生们接受新华社采访合影

留学生们一起去处理样品

曲周科技小院的学生与非洲留学生交流学习经验

留学生在德众科技小院学习巨峰葡萄种植技术

Bilisuma 在三百亩试验基地开展田间试验

Saturnin 向农业农村部前部长余欣荣同志汇报
曲周实践教育

留学生 Satumin 与 Chagga 在前衙科技小院与村里的小朋友进行互动

留学生一起观察大豆长势　　　　　　　　留学生与崔振岭教授一同见证收获的喜悦

留学生给曲周第四疃镇中小学生开展科普教育　　留学生在实验站完成科普教育后的合影

留学生在育苗园区合影

留学生在自己做的展板前庆祝活动取得成功

前衙科技小院院长李惠丽向非洲留学生
讲述小院的发展历程

萨图宁和中国学生一起记录试验数据

申建波教授与留学生在曲周实验站深入交谈

辛启来的王庄村农户试验田收获啦

2019级非洲留学生召开民主生活会

留学生为参赛葡萄打分

江荣风教授与Christina在果园合影

留学生给盆栽试验浇水

中非科技小院研究生为四疃镇中小学生做科普教育

Aminu 与小男孩合影

Jasper 在进行开题答辩

中非科技小院留学生在王庄农户示范田中

张宏彦教授为留学生讲述甜叶菊绿色种植技术

2019级留学生参加中国农业大学大学生社会活动

2019级留学生参观曲周县博物馆